P9-DIZ-738

Reflections

REFLECTIONS

Charles Rich

ST. BEDE'S PUBLICATIONS
Petersham, Massachusetts

Assoc of Hebrew Catholics
PO BOX 980280
YPSILANTI MI 48198

Copyright © 1986 by Charles Rich
All Rights Reserved
PRINTED IN THE UNITED STATES OF AMERICA

Nihil Obstat: Rev. Adam D. Schmitt
Censor Librorum

Imprimatur: +Leo A. Pursley, D.D.
Bishop of Fort Wayne-South Bend
August 5, 1976

The Nihil Obstat and Imprimatur are official declarations that a book is considered to be free of doctrinal and moral error. It is not implied that those who have granted the Nihil Obstat and Imprimatur necessarily agree with the contents, opinions or statements expressed.

Most Scripture texts used in this work are taken from the New American Bible, copyright © 1970 by the Confraternity of Christian Doctrine, Washington, D.C., and used by permission of the copyright owner. All rights reserved.

LIBRARY OF CONGRESS CATALOGING IN PUBLICATION DATA

Rich, Charles.
Reflections.

Originally published: Huntington, Ind. : Our Sunday Visitor, c1977.
1. Meditations.   I. Title.
BX2182.2.R49   1986   242   86-17732
ISBN 0-932506-49-6

St. Bede's Publications
Box 545
Petersham, MA 01366

Contents

INTRODUCTION

The author of Reflections *is a convert from Judaism who since his conversion has sought to lead a contemplative life while not being separated from the world. He has shared the results of his meditations with a few intimate friends, and it is these that make up this book. Some have appeared previously in* Our Sunday Visitor *under the pen name of Paul Davidson. Not long after his conversion, in obedience to his spiritual director, he wrote an account of his conversion which was published anonymously in* America *(June 3, 1933). It is reprinted here as an introduction to these meditations.*

Dear Father:

I am very much afraid that what you ask of me is impossible. How can I tell you what made me become a Catholic, how can I ever hope to put down on paper all that went on in my mind and heart up to the time of my conversion? What I can do is to repeat again some of the things about myself with which you are already familiar. You know, for instance, that I was raised in a strictly orthodox Jewish environment, that I had been deeply instructed in the faith of my people, and that all this training had been completely worn away by the time I had reached the age of fourteen. From then on I looked elsewhere for spiritual nutriment, in the field of culture and education.

The more culture and education I acquired, however, the more conscious I became that these would never fill the gap which the loss of my religious faith had left. It was this realization which was responsible for my preoccupation during the course of many years with the faiths and beliefs of other people, preoccupations which ultimately led me into the writings of Catholicism.

Here in Catholicism I discovered a world molded along lines which were closest to the desires of my heart; here I found a view of life which satisfied the many sides of my nature. I began to read all the great writers I could find on Catholicism, from St. Augustine's "City of God" to Karl Adam's "Spirit of Catholicism." In these books I found living waters at which I quenched my thirst for the supernatural and the Divine, a thirst which was implanted in me ever since I can remember.

Influenced as I became by the spirit of these writings, I still felt very far from the kind of Catholicism which I now know since my conversion. There were far too many qualifications to be made, too many difficulties to be overcome for me to have felt entirely at home in it. It was one thing to see the land of peace from the mountain's shaggy top and to find a way thither, and another to essay through ways unassailable and to keep on the way that leads thither.

In the meantime my spiritual and intellectual life became anarchic and chaotic; I did not know where I was, what I believed or where I stood on any matter. I felt that something desperate had to be done if I would avert spiritual suicide. I read the New Testament and tried to fathom the full meaning of Our Lord's sayings. I felt that there was something about these utterances with which I was deeply in sympathy and which was different from anything ever spoken by a human being, different in tone from the utterances of the great poets I admired so much. There was a note of hope in them, of confidence and trust which became medicinal to a mind tormented and distracted by anxiety and doubt. But in spite of the healing influence which the reading of the Gospel writings had upon me, there was yet, I felt, something vitally lacking. I was still searching. Christ had not yet become God to me. I regarded Him as but a man, a supereminently perfect and august man, this and no more. I was still under the influence of the view which Renan and the rationalist school represented. I sought elsewhere for God.

I went to Spinoza. For two years I was under the complete sway and influence of this man's mind. His Ethics had become a Bible to me. I began to worship him as a saint. The mere sound of his name would thrill me with joy. He became to me the divine, the blessed, the truly "God-intoxicated" Spinoza. And all this while I did not realize that I was worshipping a weak human being, as feeble and helpless as myself.

This drunken fury with the doctrines of pantheism lasted, as I have mentioned, for over two years. The whole universe became Spinozistic. God became everything and nothing. He was everywhere and nowhere, and I awoke from this hallucination to find myself more miserable than ever. Spinozism had failed to remove the doubt, the torment, and the anxiety that oppressed my mind; its charm faded completely, its doctrines became cold and lifeless.

What was I to do now? Where was I to turn with any hope? I lost faith in all philosophy. I turned in my desperation to the writings of the mystics, to Eckhart, to Bohme, to Plotinus and Emerson, but here I met with even greater disappointment. Under the maze of confused words which concealed their doctrines lay nothing but obscurity and darkness. The further I waded into them, the more hopelessly entangled everything became; they only led me deeper into the darkness from which I sought to emerge.

I withdrew from my acquaintances also. They were themselves too miserable to be able to afford comfort to others. And to look to them for guidance or help would be like asking the blind to lead the blind.

One day while I was passing a church, the thought occurred to me to go in and rest a while; perhaps this would bring some relief to my mind. It was not my first visit to a Catholic church; I had often been in one before, but it was the first time that I went into one with the hope of finding in there something which I could find nowhere else. And as I sat in the peace and quiet of that atmosphere these thoughts kept running through my mind:

If only I could believe with the same assurance as those who come to worship here believe! If I could only believe that the words in the Gospels are really true, that Christ really existed, and that these words are exactly those that came from His own mouth, were uttered from His own human lips, and that they are literally true. Oh, if this were only a fact, if I could only believe that this were a fact, how glorious and wonderful that would be, how consoled, happy, and comforted I would be, to know and to believe that Christ was really Divine, that He was God's own Son come down from another world to this earth to save us all! Could it be possible, I felt, that that which seemed too wonderful to be true actually was true, that it was no deception, no fraud, no lie? All of a sudden something flashed through my mind and I heard these words spoken in it. "Of course it is true, Christ is God, is God come down to make Himself visible in the flesh. The words in the Gospels are true, literally true."

The next thing I remember was that I found myself on my knees in fervent prayer and thanksgiving. I felt a deep gratitude in my heart for something which made me feel very happy, but what it was I could not say. All that I know is that from that day on the name of Our Lord Jesus Christ took on a significance which it never before had. There was an ineffable fragrance about the words *Jesus Christ*, a sweetness with which nothing can be compared. The sound of these words to this day fills me with a strange inexpressible joy, a joy which I feel does not come from this world.

It was not long after this that I saw an announcement of a series of conferences to be given by you at the Fordham University Chapel. The title, "The Mystical Christ and The Modern World," immediately captured my imagination, and I resolved to hear you the following Sunday. It was soon after this that the thought of entering the Church seriously entered my mind. I was spiritually homeless, and what better thing could I do than to ally myself with a people with a whole viewpoint with which I already had so much in common? I could accept Christ, then why not Catholicism also? After hearing you say that the Catholic Church was "Jesus Christ diffused and communicated," I was convinced that the next logical step was to embrace Catholicism.

But no sooner had I arrived at this decision than thousands of difficulties began to present themselves. I would take too long now to enter into the nature of these. Thanks to God's grace they were all successfully met.

When some of my friends learned of this intention of mine to enter the Catholic Faith they assumed a very abusive and hostile attitude toward me. Some even went so far as to warn me of serious mental disturbances unless I immediately desisted from preoccupying myself with Catholic writings. I was forfeiting, they warned me, all sound reason and I had better wake up.

This made me very sad, for I knew from what ignorance and blindness they spoke. Most of them never read a good Catholic book in their lives; their knowledge of Catholicism rested on the flimsiest sort of material gathered from wild hearsay and rumor, and the truth of the following words came forcibly home to me: "Religion has nothing more to fear than not being properly understood." It was their essential ignorance of the profound Catholic teachings that made them hate me for my willingness to embrace these teachings. It was ignorance and ignorance alone that spoke in them.

One evening while riding home on the subway, perplexed by doubt, just after having had a bitter dispute with one of my friends, the consequences of which filled me with an unbearable grief, suddenly in the midst of all this despair and darkness I felt an unaccountable feeling of happiness come over me and flood my whole inner being with joy almost heavenly. Grief instantly left me, and my anxieties and doubts vanished as if by a miracle. I knew and felt from that minute that I would be able to overcome all the obstacles in the way of my accepting Catholicism. And I did overcome them. By the aid of His light which came to me, the road became easier and easier, and on the feast of St. Cyril of

Jerusalem, March 18, 1933, I was formally received into the Church.

From then on there is little to be said. I have since my Baptism and First Communion acquired a happiness which I would not exchange for anything in all the world. It has given to me a peace of mind and a serenity of outlook which I did not think was possible on this earth. All my anxieties, doubts, and mental torments have completely left me, and I am for the first time in many years at peace with myself and with the world. I suppose the Buddhist would characterize this sort of peace by the word *Nirvana*, but I would much prefer to call it by the familiar language of Paul: "The peace of God that surpasseth all understanding."

THE MYSTERY OF OUR OWN BEING

"I give you thanks that I am fearfully, wonderfully made" (Psalm 139:14). In these words we are given a kind of hint that we should be astonished at the contemplation of our being, and that upon due reflection we should thank God for having fashioned us in such an amazing way. In the Psalmist's eyes, we are all living miracles—there is nothing ordinary for him about a human being, but something truly extraordinary. Saint Augustine has more than once reminded us that all things in the world are miracles but we cease to marvel at them because of their frequent occurrence. In Psalm 139 this thought is made clear and evident, since the very words used there in speaking of man denote something extraordinary. God wants us to marvel at ourselves, and so He has inspired the Psalmist to write the way he did. What these words try to point out is the fact that a human being will always remain an inexhaustible source of wonder to the devout and reflecting mind. No matter how much we may know about ourselves, we will never cease to be the astonishing fact that we are.

A great American religious genius said these words: "Man is a mystic fact" (Isaac Thomas Hecker, Founder of the Paulist Fathers). In this psalm practically the same thing is being reiterated, for in it we are told that in the making of man God performed a marvelous accomplishment—we are all living wonders and living miracles to ourselves. In this psalm, we are bidden to praise God and thank Him for the great mystery of all that we are—both body and soul. We are unfathomable. The deeper we delve into our peculiar makeup, the more incomprehensible we become to ourselves. There is something divine in every human being, and so this will never be able to be fathomed in the present life. "What is man," the sacred writer asks, "of what worth is he? The good, the evil in him, what are these?'' (Sirach, 18:6). The answer to this question has thus far not been forthcoming. It will not be until we are in heaven.

It is the aim of all the saints both to seek and find God in everything. However, this is especially the case in reference to their own being. The saints sought for Christ in themselves, that is why they became so sweetly enamored at the mystery of their own being. The Psalmist most certainly was seeking in Psalm 139, since he there speaks of himself as being an object of wonder and amazement to himself. We should all look at ourselves in the divine light that is Christ; thus regarded, we will perceive something in ourselves we could never have thought to be there—something truly marvelous and truly divine. Being fashioned in the divine image, man is something fundamentally different from anything else God has made. He, man, is something which he will for all eternity never cease to marvel at and wonder at and thank God for. Man will for all eternity be a sweet mystery of divine love. Who are we, and what are we? we should often prayerfully ask ourselves. The answer that will be given to this question can never be comprehended in the present life. And yet it is God's will that we should continually put this question to ourselves, since by our so doing we will identify ourselves with the holy angels.

Sanctity is attained by asking questions to which we will receive an answer after this life is over. By not asking these questions, we remain glued to time. To love God, we must always strive to seek mystery in things, but especially in our own selves. This mystery is there, and we have but to plumb the depths in which it is perceived. There is a line in the Psalms which reads, ''Deep calls unto deep'' (Ps. 42:8). This depth resides in the soul of every human being; by our probing and delving into it, we will find that for which the heart craves, something eternal and undying. We have been made for a destiny that cannot be attained in time. By reflecting upon ourselves, we shall arrive at an understanding or the perception and the awareness of the wondrousness of our makeup. In our so doing, we shall rejoice with a joy so great that we will be impelled to thank God for the miracle of our being.

We should thank God for the marvelousness of our nature, since it is as the result of His love that it came to be. God holds us in the hollow of His hand, and that hollow is the miracle that it is, but another name for the wonder and amazement the Psalmist says we all are. We look at ourselves, and as we do so we are baffled as to who and what we are. Now reflection begins with this bafflement, as well as prayer, meditation and contemplation. If more people were baffled by the mystery of their own being, there would be more saints in the world. We become saints by cultivating in ourselves a sense of wonder. Mystery leads to God, and that is why the devil hates it so much.

LOVE WITHOUT LIMITS

"When you pass through the water, I will be with you; in the rivers you shall not drown. When you walk through the fire, you shall not be burned" (Isaiah 43:2). These words are a wonderful assurance that no matter what we may have to go through in this life, it will be no source of permanent harm to the soul. Nothing can injure the essential part of our makeup except sin alone; pain cannot do this, these words tell us, and neither can suffering of any kind. In fact, pain and suffering, yes, death itself, serve but to enrich our nature, their purpose being to exalt us in Christ. Was there ever anyone who genuinely loved God and who failed to be enriched in soul by all he had to go through? How can anything in this life be a source of harm with God around to watch over us? Does it not say in the Psalms that "no evil shall befall you, nor shall affliction come near your tent" (Psalm 91:10)? These consoling words are addressed to every human being who bears the love of truth in his heart, since such a person has the Redeemer of the universe for his close Companion and Friend. God is not only a Friend to us but the Lover spoken of in the Song of Songs. As one who bears such deep affection, He is always at our side. It was the realization that this is so that prompted the "sweet singer of Israel" to compose the most beautiful words that have ever been written. "The Lord is my shepherd," he says, and so, "I shall not want" (Ps. 23:1). The remainder of this psalm is too well known to have to be quoted. God wants us to rely on Him, and this in every single need that can come up in this life. "When you pass through the water, I will be with you," He says to each one of us, and "water" in Hebrew is a figure of tribulation. We have no need to be afraid of what lies ahead of us in the future, and this no matter how dire and terrible it may be. What we should be afraid of is the fear that God will not be around to succor us in our every need.

It was God's love that brought us into our present existence, and so it will be this same love that will take us out of it. "I shall die of death," Saint Therese said when the thought came to her of her final departure from this life. It is natural to fear death; it is supernatural to rely on God's special help at such an awesome and solemn time. "When you walk through the fire, you shall not be burned." With faith in the infinite goodness of Almighty God, what is there to fear on the part of a reasonable human being? All throughout the sacred Scriptures we have been assured of the deep incomprehensible love God has for us. With this in view, how can we have any misgivings as to the final outcome of our lives? It is due to God's goodness that we were born; it is due to His goodness that we shall die and continue on existing after this life is over.

Would God have gone to the trouble of suffering and dying for us for the sake of a few years of our earthly life? He had our eternity in view when He made us out of nothing. We have nothing to fear from anything that God allows to take place in our lives, be this terrible as it may. The saints were tortured and slain, but that part of themselves destined to live forever, was unable to be harmed. Nothing external to us can do us any harm, but only what is internal. In that respect, no one can harm us except our own selves. The saints were not afraid of suffering and death. They knew it was by such means that they would go to heaven.

God loves us and the proof of this love is the fact of our having been born. Our existence is testimony to the esteem in which we are held by Him—not esteem only, but the most intense kind of affection we are able to conceive. Someone said that if we could now know the full extent of God's love for us we would die of the joy and delight such knowledge would produce in the soul. "I have loved thee with an everlasting love," God says to each one of us by the mouth of His prophet (Jeremiah 31:3). We cannot doubt the love God has for us. Every minute of our earthly life is the refutation of such a doubt. It is only when we get to heaven that we will fully comprehend the love God has had for us all the time we had been in this life. From the cradle to the grave, there are ten thousand ways by which this love is made clear and manifest. In everything that takes place in our lives, we are given a token of the esteem and affection in which we are held by God. "Can a mother forget her infant, be without tenderness for the child of her womb? Even should she forget, I will never forget you" (Is.49:15). God can never forget us but we can forget God and stop reciprocating the love He has from all eternity had for our immortal souls.

As so many have already observed, there is only one tragedy in this life—the lack of love for Him who is Love in Essence. "An ox knows its owner, and an ass its master's manger; but Israel does not know, my people have not understood (Is. 1:3). That Christ is not known is the cry of lamentation uttered by him who foretold His coming into this world. God, as it were, holds out His hand to every human being in order to lift up that human being to His own divine heights. It is this refusal on the part of men to respond to God's love that makes "the whole head sick and the heart faint" (Is. 1:5). If we truly love God we don't have to be afraid of anything, since He has a way of converting everything that happens for the greater good of our spiritual well-being. It's not for time that we have been made, and so it's not what benefits us in this life that God has in view—His concern is for what will be a source of joy to us in the world to come. Bodily pleasures are of little avail to make the soul happy, and so it's for this reason we suffer in the flesh.

NOTHING WITHOUT CHRIST

At the head of the universe stands Christ the Lord. "I am the first and the last," He says through the mouth of the Prophets, and the Patriarchs too, since we find Saint Irenaeus telling us that the "words of Moses are the words of Christ."

We cannot help ourselves without God, since we are dependent upon Him for everything. We cannot move a finger without His consent, His power, goodness and love. It is in the realization of this that our whole earthly happiness lies.

Too many take for granted what is a gift from on high. They fail to realize that everything they have and are is due to God's goodness and that without that goodness they would not even exist. Our sanctification lies in thanking God all the time. Every minute we live, we have to be aware that it's He, Christ the Lord of the universe, who enables us to do so. With this in view, namely, such a favor from heaven, how can we fail to think of Christ all the time? "All my being shall say, O Lord, who is like to you" (Ps.35:10).

The Hebrew for "being" connotes "bones," and "bones" in turn denote substance. Everything about ourselves makes us realize it's to Christ we owe what we have and are. This is the reason we have to have the thought and feeling constantly in ourselves. It's in this having the thought and feeling of Christ constantly in ourselves that our whole sanctification lies—and with this sanctification, our peace and happiness of soul. We cannot be happy unless we are saints, and we cannot be saints unless we think of Christ all the time. By thinking of Him, it's not the mind alone that's involved, since the Jews of old made no distinction between the mind and heart, but our whole being, both body and soul.

God is in ourselves, and with Him the Son and the Holy Spirit.

We have to have the Trinity in ourselves, in order that in such a way we can become incorporated into the Godhead. We cannot be happy in this life unless we feel ourselves completely belonging to Him from whom we have derived the existence we have. The saints thought of Christ all the time. It was in this thinking of Him that their happiness lay. Creatures are good, but they cannot instill into our deep inner being what God alone is able to infuse into it—His own divine sweet self. We cannot live without Christ any more than we are able to live without breathing—at least the saints felt this to be so.

We have to imitate the saints in this respect and feel ourselves unable to exist without the thought of our divine Lord dominating our every spiritual and bodily instinct. It is this mystical embrace of the Lord of the universe who is Christ in which our whole salvation lies. Men look for happiness in this life, but they seek for it in vain outside the happiness which in essence Christ is. God is happiness itself. It is to Him we have to go to become the blessed human beings that it is His will we should be.

We have been born for the blessedness Christ is, and this now, in this life, and forever afterwards. We cannot cease thinking of Him who, from the first day we have been born, has meant so much to us. We cannot get along without Christ. Those who try to do so end up in futility. "Vanity of vanities, says Qoheleth, vanity of vanities! All things are vanity" (Ecclesiastes 1:1). All is vain without the thought of the Lord of the universe constantly in our mind and heart. Too often we hear of someone taking his own life because he could find no meaning in the universe. Of course the universe has no meaning without the Lord of it to endow it with the significance it has. How anyone can go on living without the thought of Christ constantly in his heart is hard for the saints to understand. They cannot comprehend how a person can go through this life and bear what they must without Christ at their side all the time. To live like rational human beings, the Lord has to be our Shepherd, in that He it is who can guide us through the many vicissitudes that can arise. We cannot face the troubles of this life without God at our side as our faithful friend. How can we do without Him through whom we are?

Christ is our All, and there can never come a time when He will cease being everything we love and are. We are part of Himself. It's in this realization that all our earthly happiness lies. If we love Christ, we have everything. Without this love, we not only have nothing, but we even are nothing. With Christ we have and are all that in God's eyes we have been destined to become—blessed and beatified human beings. Thus blessed and beatified, we have our heaven right here on earth, at least a portion of it.

THE KINGDOM OF LOVE

"Your kingdom is a kingdom for all ages" (Psalm 145:13).

There is only one kind of sovereignty as far as God is concerned, one kind of kingdom and domain, and that is the kingdom of love, supernatural and divine love. Everything that happens to us can be explained from this principle alone, and without the understand of what love is, nothing has any meaning or significance on this earth. God's love for man is the solution to all problems. It alone is able to account for everything that takes place. "With age-old love I have loved you," God says to us by the mouth of His Prophet (Jeremiah 31:3). It is not for a day or a year or even a whole lifetime that God wishes we should be completely His, but forever and ever. And so, the only reason why we have to go through all we do is the fact that, loving us as He does, the purpose for which we have been created shall one day be accomplished, that of being the happy subjects of His kingdom of love, and this forever and ever. "God is love," the beloved disciple tells us. He is that eternal love of which His kingdom consists. He wishes to dominate by no other means than that which constitutes His essential Self-eternal Love which has been made flesh for our sake, so that by means of the Incarnation we may be transformed into the kingdom that this Love itself is.

"Your kingdom is a kingdom for all ages" (Ps.145:13). It certainly must be evident to all that these words have reference to that blessed kingdom of love which is Christ, and which same kingdom, having had no beginning, will never have an end, since He who constitutes this kingdom is eternal, namely, "Jesus Christ . . . the same yesterday, today and forever" (Hebrews 13:8). He and no other is a kingdom for all ages. For as God is love, and Christ is God, the love He is must be everlasting as Himself. Hatred, which is the kingdom of Satan, will have an end with the end of all things, but the love which is God will go on existing, since it is a kingdom for all ages. For all eternity, the kingdom that love is will dominate the hearts of all the just, whereas those who are not under its blessed sway will vanish as the Psalmist declares when he tells us that the "wicked shall not stand nor shall sinners, in the assembly of the just" (Ps. 1:5). The wicked vanish; they are brought to naught for the lack of that love which God is, and which alone is able to endow them with the principle of the life that shall last forever. Without love there can be no real and true life, since He whom the Scriptures designates by that name is the Source and Origin of all life. He is life, the only kind that has a right to be so called.

"Your kingdom is a kingdom for all ages." What is there that this kingdom does not include in itself—this kingdom of Christ that love is? What is there, what beauty, that the love of God does not embrace? If we have love, we have God, and with Him all things, seeing that He is their underlying essence. Death is the entrance into the kingdom of God, for though we may have some perception of what this kingdom is while we are in the body, we cannot fully possess its hidden inner riches until we die. It was with this in view, the necessity we have of undergoing our bodily dissolution before being able to enter into God's kingdom, that our Lord said to those about Him, "What little sense you have! . . . Did not the Messiah have to undergo all this so as to enter into his glory?" (Luke 24:25-26). In these words God Himself wishes to point out that there is no entering into His eternal kingdom of love and bliss until by means of the sufferings we have to go through we will have 'paid the last penny" (Matthew 5:26) which our sins have incurred. It is only after this has taken place, after this life is over, that we will be able to say to God, "Your kingdom is a kingdom for all ages," for we shall then see that the happiness, which we shall by means of death have entered, will never have an end anymore, since when that will occur, "the God of heaven will set up a kingdom that shall never be destroyed" (Daniel

2:44). We shall then see that God is a king forever and that His empire of love is eternal.

There is a certain sense in which everyone who loves God may be said to be a king, in that he is set over the empire of the inner riches his soul contains. By acts of faith, hope and love, we can all be sovereigns of our own souls, and thus rule over an empire whose extent exceeds the bounds of time. What is one beautiful thought when compared with the paltry goods of something finite? What are all things temporal to Him whose kingdom extends to the things of the next life? What is a king of earth compared to Him whose goods are heavenly and spiritual, and thus immune to the ravages of time? The kingdom over which the Christian rules is that ageless eternity that never had a beginning. It consists in that infinite and inexhaustible wealth of unseen treasures that Christ is. Why weep for a world that passes away? Why lament that "stones fall and men die?" (St. Augustine). Have we not been assured by God Himself that "If there is a natural body, be sure there is also a spiritual body" (I Cor. 15:44).

Throughout the whole of Scripture God speaks of His kingdom, the "promised land" into which He intends one day to bring us all. "The Lord is my shepherd," the Psalmist says (Ps. 23:1) and by this he means that God governs us by means of His love. Love is the only kind of dominion with which He wishes to sway the hearts of men—it is the only empire over which He wishes to be king. Christ wants to be the king of love and by its means to subjugate us to His kingdom. The Psalmist, having foreknown this, says, "Your kingdom is a kingdom for all ages" (Ps. 145:13). Being divinely inspired, he knew that the love with which God loves shall have no end.

THE CHURCH IS OUR CONFIDENCE

The Church is our Mother and God is our Father, so we have nothing to worry about, nothing to fear from the forces of evil that go prowling about the world. The Church is with us from the cradle to the grave, and with her around, what is there to dismay and disconcert us in this life?

I was for many years not a Catholic, and now that I look back, I wonder how I managed to endure what I did. It's impossible for us to realize in the present life all we owe to Mother the Church, guarding as she does our spiritual and intellectual life. She does so that we may not be victimized by the error and deceit with which the world is filled.

Centuries ago there was a saying that he who does not have the Church for his Mother cannot have God for his Father. In all essentials, this is still true in this our so-called enlightened modern age—enlightened not in the truth of things but in error, so much that we need a guide to steer us from the shoals.

Even as far back as the time of Moses, we find error creeping into God's revealed truths pertaining to the salvation and sanctification of the soul. How much more is this true today with accumulating error as history rolls on. Every day men's minds add to these errors and untruths, and so we have to have an institution like the Church of Rome to steer us clear of them, and in this way to make for us a safe passage from time to eternity. The Church is the Mother of our spiritual and intellectual life, and so, without her at our side, we have no way of knowing for certain what is true and what is false in our thinking processes. It's no wonder then that there are so many misguided souls in the world today without her to direct them aright.

We need the Church in the same way as a child need a grown-up person to guide and educate him. Just as Moses led the people of Israel out of their Egyptian bondage, so we have need of the Church to set us free from the intellectual enslavement of the errors of men's minds. From how many false philosophical systems has not the Church set us free!

Those who are born into the Church take so much for granted. It's the outsider, whom God's grace has brought into her, who really appreciates all she is meant by God to be in his spiritual and intellectual life. "Hold nothing in greater honor than your entrance into the Church," someone said. The Church of Rome is always at our side. It's in this, her being close by, that our whole security lies.

The Church of Rome is the peace of Christ of which the Scriptures speak. She is the "promised land" which Moses saw from afar; it's of her he prophesied. Mystically she is the "land flowing with milk and honey" into which God said He would bring the people of Israel. One cannot say enough about the wonderfulness of the organization known as the Catholic Church, seeing she has her roots in eternity. On our way out of this world, may it be our grace to say what the great Saint Teresa did: "After all, I am a daughter of the Church." There is no substitute for the Church of Rome—it is in vain we will seek outside of her what is meant by God to be had in her alone. There is a flood about us in which men are drowned, and this flood consists of error and falsehood. Without the Rock she is on, upon which to anchor our hearts and minds, we will be swept away into spiritual and intellectual confusion, into that "darkness and gloom" of which Job speaks (Job 10:21).

THANKSGIVING IS A GRACE

If we were sufficiently reflective, we would be so busy thanking God that we would have no time left for any other occupation. Saint Therese said that "everything is a grace." Literally, everything. All that happens to us from the day of our birth until our entry into heaven which death is, in all these things God's goodness and love in our regard is made manifest. No matter what happens to us, pleasing or displeasing, viewed from the point of view of the life to come, it will turn out to be an inestimable treasure from on high. What are all the joys we have experienced on earth compared with those we shall yet have after our departure from this life? An eternity of joy awaits us as soon as we close our eyes in death. And so, when we think of this, what else is there in this life worth doing save to thank God? The saints thanked God all the time and for everything that took place in their lives. To be what they have been, we must do the same.

At the end of our life we will be amazed to see how everything God allowed to take place in our lives was a means of bringing us closer to union with Himself. Pain as well as pleasure is a means of divine union when viewed from the perspective of the life to come. Everything that occurs does so for the purpose of procuring for us a good that will last forever. God is a mystery, but He is a mystery of goodness and love, a goodness and love that has no bounds set to it and extends beyond the limits of human comprehension. We cannot comprehend God's goodness to us; if we could, we would die, the joy of such an experience forcing the soul to leave the body. Saint John of the Cross tells us that men die for joy as well as of grief, and so the knowledge of God's goodness to us would become the cause of our death. From how many perils to body and soul have we not already been set free? From how many such perils are we not yet to be rescued as long as we shall remain in this life? All this we owe to God's goodness in our behalf. It is for this reason we can never cease thanking Him. Gratitude to God for all He has already done for us will always constitute the basis of true holiness of life and genuine sanctity. Without thankfulness we can never be pleasing to God, and neither can we be happy. To be truly at peace we have to call to mind all that God has already done for us and thank Him accordingly. By giving thanks, we shall lay up for ourselves those "treasures in heaven" spoken of by our Lord. A thankful heart serves to neutralize the pain and anguish which must sooner or later be experienced by every human born into this world.

"The favors of the Lord I will sing forever," the Psalmist says (89:1). What these "favors" are every reasonable human being is able to understand. They consist in our having been born into this life, as well as the graces we shall receive on our departure from it. Just as it is a grace to have been born, so also is it a grace to die and by means of death to enter into the "joys of the Lord." Earthly life is a good, great and wonderful thing, but the one in heaven is infinitely more so. It is for these "favors" we thank the Lord. We thank God for our bodies as well as for our souls, both being the manifestation of His goodness to us. We also thank Him for the events and circumstances of our lives, be these good or bad, pleasing or displeasing, painful or joyous. We thank God for everything, thus rendering ourselves worthy of admiration by the holy angels. By thanking God in all the circumstances of our lives, we enlarge our hearts, thus increasing their capacity for His own kind of joy to be poured into them. Who is there that does not love a thankful heart? Who does not disdain a melancholy and ungrateful one? Let us become like Christ by being thankful to His Father in heaven. It was God who took care of us when we were yet little children. The same Lord it will be who shall watch over us when we grow old. God is always on the lookout for our interests and well-being, and this in spite of the fact that to our limited view this seems sometimes the contrary.

"Give thanks to the Lord, for he is good," we are told in the Psalms (Psalm 107:1). Many things seem baffling to us because we fail to remember that we have not been made for this life alone. It is in this, God's thinking of the good of our soul, that His goodness is made manifest, and for which concern gratitude should fill our hearts. It is not for a few moments of time that we were made to live but for what follows upon our departure from this life. It is the good of that life God has in view when He allows things to occur in which we can see no good. He allows us to suffer so that we may be purified from what is contrary to union with Himself. God loves us too much for Him not to allow that to happen which, from a merely natural point of view, we feel should never have occurred.

We cannot understand the reasons for things in the present life and it is precisely for this inability to understand them that we should be grateful to God, since they appear to us all the more wonderful insofar as we do not understand them. God allows mystery to exist because without it our life in this world would become unendurable. What would become of all art, all poetry, and all religious phenomena without the sense of mystery pervading their domain as its natural habitat? We should thank God for allowing us to be ignorant of things which, from a merely natural point of view, we believe we should understand. It is in this sense that we should thank God for everything, for everything we now know and everything we now don't know but shall know in our home in heaven.

We should thank God for everything we are in body and soul, as well as for everything we will yet be in body and soul in the state of glory. We cannot be thankful enough is the refrain of the saints. Both in adverse and favorable circumstances the saints thanked God. To be what they were, we must do the same. "Curse God and die," Job's wife said to her saintly husband. But what was the answer she received? ''We receive good things from God; and shall we not accept evil?'' (Job 2:9-10). The saints thanked God all the time for everything and in everything. They did so because they knew that God causes everything to work for their eternal well-being. The saints did not live for time alone but for its eternal counterpart. We too must seek our eternal well-being, and we do so by thanking God for everything He allows to happen to us. The spirit of gratitude will produce in us the kind of joy that will never have an end. If we realized all we owe to God, we would die of the confusion such a realization brought with it. If we fully knew all we owe to God, we would never stop thanking Him every minute of our lives, this thanking Him rendering us unfit for any other preoccupation. It is gratitude to God that makes us saints, there being nothing else we can do that has such efficacy in itself.

MAN, THE MICROCOSM

Christ is the divine sun illuminating the heaven that is holiness. In the soul of each human being there is an entire universe which is irradiated by the glory of God. When we have the grace to penetrate into our inner being, we have already in a way entered into eternity. There is in each of us a world all its own, and when we penetrate into it we enter into what we shall be fully absorbed in after this life is over.

For the saints eternity begins here on this earth, so that they in that way get a taste of the joys that are there. "Taste and see how good the Lord is" (Psalm 34:9). There is a sweetness about the things of the next life with which nothing on earth can be compared. It is in our longing after that sweetness that we are rendered pleasing to God. We often neglect our inner selves, and for this reason we have no living experience of the things of Christ.

Christ Himself wishes to be our life. It is He who wishes to illuminate us with the light of His human and divine personality. And so, just as there is a heaven above that we see with the eyes of our body, so there is a celestial stellar system deep within the soul of every human being. We enter therein by God's grace.

There is a beauty about the soul of a human being the full extent of which we shall only be able to appreciate after this life is over. The saints lived in two worlds, the world within and the one without. To know what God is like we have to imitate them in this respect.

There is something wonderful about a human being, and this is due to the fact that he has in himself something of God's own wonderfulness. There is a heaven of ineffable delight in the soul of each human being, and so we have but to ask for the grace to be able to delve into ourselves for that delight to be experienced. "Taste and see how good the Lord is'' (Psalm 34:9). Taste the inner riches of your own being and you will soon get an idea of the infiniteness of God's own bliss. We become partakers of that bliss by entering deep into the inner richness of our own blessed selves. Are we not all blessed with the blessedness that Christ is? We are, and there is a wealth of beauty in ourselves to be had for the taking.

It is not for nothing our Lord said, ''The reign of God is already in your midst'' (Lk. 17:21). The tragedy is that so many pass themselves by without as much as taking a glance of all that they are in the eyes of God. There is a mystical something in the soul of a human being, but it cannot be grasped without the aid of God's grace. Once this grace is extended to us we behold in ourselves the universe we are, the world of inner riches, with the center of that world being Christ the Lord. Our human nature is idealized in Christ, so that what He is, we may all one day be.

THE VALUE OF SUFFERING

Years ago, quoting Saint Teresa, my revered and learned spiritual director said these words to me: "To labor and to pray is a good way to serve God, but to suffer is better." I have been unable to locate the exact place in the writings of Saint Teresa where these words occur, but it does not matter since I have never been able to eradicate the message from my deep inner being. Suffering is a mystery, but it's a mystery of the God-Man who willed to save the world by its means, as well as to reopen the gates of paradise closed by sin. We cannot get to heaven unless we embrace the Cross in the innumerable aspects of it that God's will presents to us. We cannot know who and what God is without the refining and purifying effects that suffering produces in the souls of men. We cannot even know what we ourselves are unless we suffer a certain amount of pain and anguish.

At the dawn of history, a sin was committed, and so the consequences of it have to be paid for, consequences which are pain of body and mind. Some people don't believe in the doctrine of original sin, yet they are unable to avoid the consequence of it in their own lives. We don't have to believe in God to be punished by Him.

Suffering is really an effect of God's love for the human race, since it is by its means we are sanctified. For those who are perplexed by the mystery of pain, there stands the Cross of Christ with the nails driven into the sacred flesh of the God-Man. Why did Christ have to suffer? What did He ever do to deserve the fate at the hands of those who, prompted by the devil, put Him to death. As for those who do not believe that the Messiah has already come, let them ask themselves why all the Patriarchs and the Prophets had to suffer. Were not these Patriarchs and Prophets among the holiest people who ever lived? Were not they all beloved by

God? Why did their loving and merciful Father in heaven permit them so much anguish of body and mind?

Suffering is an enigma, but an enigma of love. God loves us, and so it's for this reason we are allowed to experience pain of body and mind. It's not for the few paltry years of the present life we have been put on earth, but for those endless ages of eternity beyond the power of human calculation. We suffer in order to be able to rejoice in the kind of deep inner spiritual delight suffering always brings with it. We suffer in time so that we may be able to rejoice in eternity. We suffer in time so as to possess one day what we cannot now have. Suffering clears away the haze from the soul's gaze, so that we may be able to perceive the invisible good things of almighty God. It is not for the few moments of our earthly state we have been born, but for endlessness. It is to make possible the joys of the life to come that God allows us to now be purified.

Christ is a suffering Messiah. In order that He should suffer, He was rejected by His own people. We too can reject Christ if we refuse to accept the pain and anguish God allows us to experience in the present life. We reject the Cross when we say to God that it's not right that we should have to suffer all that we do in our present earthly state. The saints became what they were by the acceptance of the Cross, and there is no other road by which we reach the home of our Father in heaven. Why suffering? Why the Cross? Why the Crucifixion? These are all deep mysteries of the Christian religion, and the answer to them will be fully had only when we get to heaven. We cannot know on earth why we have to suffer all that we do. We can only look at the Crucifix and say "Amen" to all God allows to take place in our lives. We cannot become saints save in the manner of the Saint of saints. What this manner is can be found in the four gospels and the Epistles of Saint Paul, yes, and even in the Old Testament writings, such as the Book of Psalms, in the prophetical writings of Isaiah and Jeremiah, the Book of Job, as well as in all the others. Reading with faith and love, we will find suffering in these books as well as the joy such suffering always brings with it.

God is infinitely just, and so for every kind of suffering He allows us to experience He provides us with a corresponding joy. Suffering deprives us of bodily pleasures, and it does so solely for the purpose of bestowing on the soul a delight to be had in no other way. We cannot know what the delight of God is unless we go through all manner of anguish. There was a time when the delight of heaven was able to be had without pain, but this was before sin was committed. To return to our former paradisal state, we have to be scorched with the fiery sword placed by God in the hands of the cherubim guarding the way of everlasting bliss (Genesis 3:24). This "fiery sword" symbolizes the pain and anguish of body and mind which has to be undergone by those who wish to know what the joys of heaven will be like. "I assure you: this day you will be with me in paradise" (Luke 23:43), God says to all those who suffer. By means of suffering we can all be other Christs and do what He himself accomplished. Pain is bitter, but what it leads to is infinitely sweet.

Most who believe in religion would like to become saints, but how many refuse to undergo the process of holiness suffering will always be! Suffering will always constitute an unavoidable experience for the lot of man. Hence, we should say with Job, "We accept good things from God; and should we not accept evil?" (Job 2:10).

It is sheer misery to be afflicted in body and soul, but we have the Son of God giving us an example in this regard. What pain and anguish did He Himself not go through? One look at a crucifix will tell us more about the meaning of suffering than ten thousand holy and noble words. It is the deed that counts as far as God is concerned and not the many nice thoughts we may happen to have regarding Him. To suffer is to act and behave in a Christlike way. It is to imitate Him in His suspension on the Cross. We are on the Cross when we suffer, and so at that time we find ourselves to be like unto His own sacred Self. Finding ourselves to be like Him, we rejoice with a joy that shall last forever.

"Suffering is the staircase to paradise," a saint said. It's the ladder on which Jacob saw the angels of God ascending and descending (Genesis 28:12). We cannot lose when we suffer; we can only gain the graces we receive as the result of that suffering. Would our Lord have suffered if there were no graces to be derived by undergoing pain of body and mind? Christ sanctified pain, thus elevating it as a means to Himself. Suffering silences the passions enabling us to hear the voice of Christ speak in our souls—the Voice saying to us that we were made for something infinitely more wonderful than the sense of the body are able to experience; the senses, that is, in their present unglorified state. The time will come when these senses will be transfigured in Christ, so that we will see and hear what they do who are now in heaven.

In his commentary on the Book of Job, Saint Gregory the Great tells us that "The present life is a road by which we journey on to our home: and we are harassed by frequent disturbances, that we may not love our road instead of our home." It's not to make us miserable that God allows us to undergo the anguish of our earthly lot. He does so with a view to our heavenly state. Suffering is bitter, but it leads to what is infinitely sweet. It leads to heaven and the divine sweetness we shall there experience. Christ came to transfigure the woes of the world, thus rendering them capable of eternal happiness. God allows no evil to exist from which He cannot derive greater glory for His elect souls.

Pain brings us to Christ by creating in ourselves a distaste for passing things. It counters this distaste with a longing for what shall endure forever. How sad the lot of those who do not have Christ to look up to in their pain and anguish? There is a terrible deficiency in the life of a person who has to suffer and is yet deprived of the consolation that the contemplation of the Cross brings to the soul. And while Christianity is a religion of suffering, it is at the same time a religion of the joy accompanying that suffering.

GOD OUR FRIEND

How good God is! And yet, ungenerous as we are, we easily give way to discouragement. God's goodness to us impels Him to concern Himself with all our interests. He is aware of our every single necessity, and He will in His own good time more than fulfill that necessity. Yet we are so easily discouraged. We fail to realize that we have the Lord of the universe for our intimate companion and friend. There are many troubles rising from our life in this world, but God's goodness and love will see us through these troubles. "When you pass through the water, I will be with you," God says to each of us, "in the rivers you shall not drown. When you walk through the fire, you shall not be burned: the flames shall not consume you" (Isaiah 43:2). With these divine words to assure us, what is there to fear in this life? God will see us through all our trials. By means of His grace they will all be overcome. How easily we give way to doubts and misgivings of every variety! "God's in His heaven— / All's right with the world," the great poet Robert Browning says. We are so fearful of the vicissitudes of this life, but where is our trust in God's infinite goodness, His mercy and love in our regard?

The devil wants us to be miserable. He hates joy and peace of heart. It is his malignant design to rob us of these. "The devil steals our good thoughts," St. Gregory the Great tells us. To whom shall we listen, to the enemy of the human race or to its friend, our Lord? We cannot let God down by worrying as to what will become of us. Each day brings us nearer to the goal of our heart's desire, the goal which is our Lord and Savior Jesus. We have been redeemed by His precious Blood. With this certainty, what is there to disconcert us in the present life? We are so tempted to worry about what will become of us as we go on living. However, we do God wrong to give way to such worry. How often have we not been assured by Him that all shall be well?

Every day, something takes place in our lives to assure us that we are loved by an infinitely good God. Every day He manifests this love and goodness to us, and this in a thousand different ways. Our salvation lies in the fact that we are loved by an infinitely merciful Lord, and our sanctification, too. God will not let us down, providing we ourselves do not do so. Many there are who do not love themselves in and with the love which is our Lord. They fail to esteem and reverence their human nature redeemed by Christ. They fail to think of the joys of heaven which by the grace of God will one day be their own. God wants us to love ourselves. He wishes we should immerse ourselves in His divine Son, since it's only in this way we can be happy and at peace in this life.

"Rejoice in the Lord," Saint Paul never tires of saying to us. What the Apostle to the Gentiles tells us is reiterated throughout the Book of Psalms. We cannot love God enough. We cannot be happy enough in Him. The longer we stay in this life the more we realize that there is nothing in it worth worrying about. Both the good and evil in it pass away. The saints were lighthearted people, due to their living in God's presence all the time. The saints were interiorly joyous, and this in spite of the external miseries in which they were so often steeped. We must think of Christ and all He has done for us by His becoming Man. God loved us, that's why we were born. Had He not loved us, we would never have been. His love is responsible for the existence we have.

Unbelievers are sad and unhappy people. They are devoid of the grace of God to render them immune to the troubles of this life. We must sing to the Lord the "new song" that the Christian religion is—the religion by which we are assured that we shall be inconceivably happy as soon as we close our eyes in death. We are happy in this life too, but not to the extent we shall then be. "I rejoiced," the Psalmist said, "because they said to me, 'We will go up to the house of the Lord' " (Ps. 122:1). It's to the joys of the next life these words have reference, and not to the one in which we now find ourselves. The saints rejoiced when they thought of death, seeing it as a means to enter into their eternal glory.

God is with us all the time, though we see Him not in the way we do other things. God is with us to console us in the sorrows we go through. There is no room for despair in the heart of a Christian—this in spite of the many evils in which he finds himself. "How great are those souls," Saint Francis de Sales says, "who amid the vicissitudes of every kind always keep their thoughts and affections fastened on eternal goodness so as to cherish it forever" (Treatise On The Love Of God, book 9, chapter 15). Instead of thinking of the troubles of this life we should center our hearts and minds on the kind of existence we shall have after we have left this world. Sinners are deprived of the joys had by those who think constantly of Christ. "Will he then delight in the Almighty and call upon Him constantly?" Job asks in reference to such people (Job 27:10).

'COME, LORD JESUS!'

This whole world and this whole life is a "prison," the Psalmist says, and so he asks God to be freed from it. "Lead me forth from prison, that I may give thanks to your name" (Ps. 142:8). It is evident from these words that we cannot adequately praise God in the present life, and this is due to the obstacles that there are to such praise. The soul now resides in a mortal body with the limitations of such a body. When death comes, we shall be freed from the restrictions to which we are now subjected. It is then alone we shall be truly free, "free among the dead," as the old Vulgate used to translate the passage in one of Psalms. All the time the saints were in this life, they longed for heaven, realizing as they did that this world was not their true home. Everything we encounter in this life has in it a mixed good, the mixed good to which we became heirs as the result of sin. Prior to the time they sinned, Adam and Eve experienced a good without any evil in it. They knew none of the woes of our present mortal state. When death comes, we shall be restored to the unmixed good once had in the paradisal state.

We cannot be completely happy in our present life, nor are we able to be fully at peace in it. It was for this reason the saints yearned for a completely different kind of existence than the one in which we now find ourselves. They gave expression to this longing in a thousand different ways. "For to me, 'life' means Christ; hence dying is so much gain" (Philippians 1:21), one of them said. It was no death wish the saints had, but a longing for the place where they were assured by their Catholic faith that they would be completely happy. It's so hard to find people longing for heaven these days, and so we have to take comfort in the realization that there always have been a few among God's friends whose main earthly desire was to be with Him in the state of glory.

We long for heaven, not because we are tired of this life, but to enjoy what they do who are already there. It's an angelic kind of existence we crave, and not the one to be had on this earth. We long for God where He can be perfectly praised and perfectly loved. For those who love God, earth is a wearisome place in which to be. It's the yearning for heaven that makes saints, and that yearning alone. The saints are not merely good people who perform acts of virtue—they are infinitely more than that. The saints are characterized by their desire to be with God in His high heaven, there to partake of His own divine joys. It's this yearning that makes saints. Works are good, but they will not obtain for the soul what sanctity alone is able to procure for it, oneness with Jesus Christ. "Woe is me that I sojourn in Mesech, that I dwell amid the tents of Kedar!" (Psalm 120:5), the Psalmist says. By "Kedar" is signified the miseries of our mortal lot. All the saints longed for heaven, and to be included in their society, we must do the same thing. With them, we must long for the time when we shall no longer be subjected to the limitations of our present bodily being, but freed from its necessities. Only then shall we be able to love God the way they do who are no longer on this earth.

There is so much suffering in this life, that it's hard to understand why we cling so tenaciously to it; why with Saint Paul we do not long to be "freed" from it in order to be with Christ, and this in the only satisfactory way it is possible to be with Him. We cannot at present praise God in the way they do who are already in heaven. The best way to pray to God is to want to be with Him in the state of glory. Was it not this Moses asked when he said to God, "Do let me see your glory!" (Ex. 33:18)? We too, want to see the glory of God, and this in a way death alone can make possible. When the saints longed for what they did, they were misinterpreted by those who did not have the grace to have such a longing in themselves. All the saints wanted to die, but they wanted to do so in perfect conformity with God's holy will in the matter. The saints never wanted anything save what it was God's will that they should have. It was not so much death the saints wanted but God's will in that death. The saints asked God to lead them forth from this life in the way and manner pleasing to Him. It was not death they desired but Christ Jesus, reached only by means of their bodily demise. The saints wanted nothing but God. It was this desire for what was exclusively divine that made the saints what they were.

The saints lived from moment to moment, doing God's will as it made itself manifest to them during that moment. God wants us to live for one moment at a time and not to be overconcerned with what tomorrow has in store. One moment at a time was the motto of the saints; it was in this way that they were able to put up with the trials of their lot. It's in the moment in which we now find ourselves that God wants us to live. There is a beautiful expression in the Epistle to the Thessalonians that has always fascinated me. It goes like this: " . . . to await from heaven the Son he (God) raised from the dead—Jesus . . . " (1 Thess. 1:10). How wonderfully these words sum up the purpose of this life! This is the objective which as Christians we should place before ourselves and the goal we should set our hearts upon. What better way to spend our earthly days than in looking forward to the coming of Christ in His glorified state? We can become saints if we say with Saint John, "Come, Lord Jesus!" (Revelation 22:20).

WEARING OLD AGE

We feel ourselves moving along as the years pass on, and it is from this that the Jews of old got their idea of "pilgrimage." This life is a journey, they tell us, and so we can never remain static from one moment to the next. Intellectually and spiritually we are always moving about from one state to another, and so the time must come when all this metaphorical moving about will have to reach an end. We will one day have to go back to God from whence we came. We came into this world in a definite period of time, and so a wise man is he who is always looking forward to the day when he will depart from it. The Jews of old never felt at home in this life, so if we would imitate their own profound insights, we would beg God for the grace to be able to do the same thing. We can't settle down in a world like this, for there is always something in it to accelerate our passage through time. Old age reminds us that we are going somewhere, and that somewhere is the blessed life to come. It's good to feel ill-at-ease in a world like this, when nothing remains the same from one moment to the next, where everything is in the state of transition and flux of which the Greeks have spoken. We are conscious of being wanderers on earth as time passes, and this is a good healthy Christian feeling. The Jews of old were overmastered by the fact that they had here no lasting city, and that's why they wrote the Old Testament Books. What are these but a description of their journey through time?

Some people mistakenly don't want to move on, and so they look upon old age as a kind of burden. Nothing disconcerts them more than the fact that they will one day be compelled to take leave of this life, and this whether they want to or not, whether they will be in the mood for doing so or not. Time is inexorable, and so it spares no one in its sweep through the years. In a spiritual way, we have to keep going until that day arrives when we are safe in our Father's house in heaven. And so, until that day, we cannot settle down in the enjoyment of that rest promised by God to all His saints. In a metaphorical way, we have to march along with the currents of time, for time will sweep everything in its path. We cannot stay forever in a world like this, and so it's good to be on the lookout for the day on which we shall have to depart from this life and exchange it for one that's infinitely more beautiful. Death will usher us into that life; that's why the thought of it should be so welcome to us and we should rejoice at the news of its approach. "I rejoiced because they said to me, 'We will go up to the house of the Lord,' " the divine Psalmist said (Psalm 122:1). These words are a perfect expression of what a truly enlightened person should feel and think on the subject of his final departure from this life; they have the right Christian tone in them. We can't improve on Scripture, for it's God's way of telling us how we should feel and think as regards the end of all things. We rejoice at the passing of our earthly years and look upon them as leading to something infinitely better than what they have to offer. Death is a welcome friend to those who love things divine.

It's much easier to meditate on death when we are old, since age renders the proximity of it more graphic and real. As we grow older we begin to feel ourselves carried away from ourselves; old age makes us conscious of that part of our makeup that will live forever, and it weakens our hold on what has to pass away with time. We have to thank God for old age as well as for youth—these two portions of our life bring with them two different types of graces. They are both good, and they should be equally loved and cherished. "Neither in my youth, nor now that I am old, have I seen a just man forsaken," the Psalmist tells us (37:25). In these words we are assured that God will in His sweet and divine way provide for our every need, and so we have nothing to worry about. God takes care of old people in the same way that He does of those who are young. He has assured us of this in a thousand different ways. "Hear me, O house of Jacob. . . . My burden since your birth, whom I have carried from your infancy. Even to your old age I am the same, even when your hair is gray I will bear you. . . . I who will carry you to safety" (Isaiah 46:3-4). We have nothing to fear from growing old, for we are in the hands of the same God who has in His mercy and love brought us forth from our mother's womb. Life is a journey which should terminate in infinite bliss.

The years bring with them a wisdom that those who are young cannot possess, for youth oftentimes means perturbation and restlessness. Young people experience a misery that's abysmal and devastating, through which no one who has once passed will in his right mind ever want to return. We become homeward bound as we grow older, and the blessed realization of this becomes a source of consolation which all the wealth in the world is unable to buy. We are going home, the years say to us, and as they do so, we rejoice in the heart. Soon the heart will stop beating, and the goal of our life will be attained—the goal God has in store for us as soon as we close our eyes in death. Death is a sweet and loving friend, and the saints held it to be tragic that it is so often mistakenly viewed. How many have the grace to have the right Christian attitude to the greatest blessing which, after our existence, God has given to the human race?

It's pleasant to think of old age and death when we love God, but it's quite the opposite when through our own fault such a grace is withheld from us. The saints loved God in everything—they were no pickers-and-choosers. That's why they were such blessed possessors of heavenly peace. Come, old age! They asked to accept it from Him as one of His choicest gifts. The saints are the only thoroughly integrated people this earth produced, for they were completely oriented to everything that took place in their lives. And so, in a certain way, they had no problems. The further away from holiness we are, the more perplexed we become, and it's this which makes old age such an unpleasant subject for some people to contemplate.

The saints looked upon old age as a means of drawing closer to God. As they saw their bodies decline, the more joyful they became. Old age is a beautiful experience to those who are saints, but quite a melancholy one for ordinary Christians. It takes grace to love growing old. To become saints, we must love everything that can happen to us from the cradle to the grave, since all that occurs does so for our greater eternal well-being. This will be clear to us in heaven. On earth, it takes great faith to realize that this is so. To be afraid of growing old is to be afraid of drawing closer to God, and the same thing holds true of everything else in this life, such as suffering and death. Youth is too passionate and unrestrained to love God purely, and so we can do this in a much better way when we receive the wisdom the years alone can bring with them. "Thank God for everything," the saints used to say, and if we would grow old gracefully, we have to give heed to their admonition. And though youth is a blessing, old age is equally so. It is a grace to bear it well.

ON BEING CATHOLIC

How fortunate we are to be able to believe in all the truths the Church teaches! How blessed not only to be able to believe in these truths but to have the grace to make the beauty of them part of our own selves! It has been said that we should love the Lord our God with our whole heart, with our whole mind and with our whole strength, indicating that the truths of the Catholic religion have to be ingrained in our inmost being, and that they become part of that being. How we shall thank God when we get to heaven for having given us the grace to believe in the only true Church! Where would we be today if we were not Catholic? What a lot of confusion and perplexity of mind we avoid by having been made members of the household of faith.

In our being Catholics we have the most important thing anyone can possess in this life. How the gift of faith compensates for whatever we fail to have that we think we should have! How can anyone who has the gift of faith complain to God for not having what he thinks essential to him? In bestowing upon us the gift of faith, has not God given us the most important thing a human being can have in this life? Is it not by means of this faith that an eternity of happiness has been assured to us? We should enter into a state of ecstasy every time we think we think of Christ and the Church He founded!

We cannot thank God enough for the gift of faith, and this if we lived an unaccountable number of years. As Catholics, what we have is priceless. It cannot be compared with anything to be found on this earth. We should rejoice and exult every time we call to mind all God has done for us by His gift of faith in our divine Lord. We should rejoice over the fact that because of His love for us we are not only Christians but Catholics as well. It is the gift of faith that should count in our lives and no other thing, be this good and beautiful as it may. How happy we should consider ourselves to be what all the saints have been, believers in our divine Lord. Is not such faith glory enough for any human being? Can anything be compared to the happiness and delight with that of being Catholics! God does not want us to die but live for this faith and share it with those around us. In giving us Himself by means of the Church what is there God has withheld from us which we think we should have?

"After all I am a daughter of the Church," Saint Teresa said on her way out of this life. To console ourselves we should always have these words in our hearts. "I am a Christian, I am a Christian," a great Jewish convert used to say to himself every time he was tempted to grow despondent over the condition of his lot (Ven. M. P. Libermann). We should say the same thing when we feel ourselves let down in this life. To be a Catholic is glory enough for any man.

KNOWING OURSELVES

There is something godlike about a human being, and this is in his intellectual and spiritual life, as well as in his ability to choose right from wrong. Man alone can reach for the heights of sublimity, thus placing himself in the category of the holy angels. "What is man," the Psalmist asks of God, "that you should be mindful of him, or the son of man that you should care for him? You have made him a little less than the angels" (Psalm 8:5-6). God has raised us to His own divine heights there to remain for all eternity. There is something marvelous about a human being, something too wonderful to be completely understood in the present life. We have to wait till we get to heaven to appreciate fully the wonder of our own nature.

Man is always bent on the effort to transcend the limits of his finite nature, and it is in this that his glory lies. His glory consists in craving for the infinite, but to have the infinite he must die. What we crave in the depth of our being cannot be had in the present life. It was for this reason that with Saint Paul all the saints said: "I long to be freed from this life and to be with Christ" (Philippians 1:23). The saints sensed something marvelous about themselves, and it was to perceive this more fully that they wanted to pass beyond the limits of their mortal nature.

The saints craved for death in order thus to be able to enjoy experiencing the wonderfulness of their own being and to comprehend the mystery of themselves.

There is something marvelous about a human being, seeing he has been made in the image of the divine nature. His spiritual life consists in this wondering about himself and the effort he makes to comprehend the mystery of himself. He looks forward to death as the means by which this may be done. "I give you thanks that I am fearfully, wonderfully

made" (Ps. 139:14). In the Hebrew, "fearfully" may be
rendered "awesomely" and "with reverence." There is a
reverent awe connected with everything about a human
being. It was for this reason that the saints said that we
should reverence ourselves. The more we reflect on our own
being, the more awesomely we appear to be, and the more
wonderful and marvelous. Who and what are we? We are
mysteries of God's divine love. We are "fearfully, wonderfully made," it is for this reason that we should never cease
thanking God. We should be grateful to Him for having
fashioned our nature like unto the one of His only-begotten
Son, thus raising us to His own divine heights. There is a
spark in us which was lighted when we were first created out
of nothing, and being divine, this spark will never go out.

There is something in ourselves akin to the angels, thus
rendering us capable of their beatific bliss—a joy that begins
on earth and never has an end. What are we? We are replicas
of the God-Man. It is in this our glory lies. It consists in our
being other Christs, living His life, thinking His thoughts, as
well as feeling the way He has done all the time He was on
this earth. We are imitators of the God-Man, and so no one
has a right to interfere in our efforts to become divinized.
Physically, we may be destroyed by evil-minded men as the
result of the efforts we make along this line, but spiritually,
all such hindrances will come to naught. The saints were put
in prison; they were killed as a result of the effort they made
to become one with the Redeemer of the universe. Men tried
to drag down the saints to their own low level, but Christ
frustrated the attempts. "Imitate our own earth-bound
aims," evil-minded men say to us. "Do not aspire to become
what God Himself is." This is the devil's own voice spoken
through the mouths of the wicked-minded.

Today more than ever, we have to listen to the voice of
Christ heard in the depth of the soul and not to His sworn
enemy. We have to reflect on the wonder of our own being
and derive the joy that ensues from such reflection. Have not
all the truly great men and women done this very thing?
Have not the great masterpieces of literature and art been

the result of such reflection? Do not all these great works evoke in ourselves the sweet sense of mystery in connection with everything we are, body and soul? We have to have a reverence for our own selves, the saints never tired saying to us, since it's by means of this reverence that we will be given the grace to realize all we are from the point of view of the life to come. We have a divine destiny, and so we should beware of exchanging it for what is less than itself. It is not downward, to what is low in ourselves, that we have to fix the gaze of our soul, but to what lies beyond the reach of our mortal limits. We must set out sights on Him who says, "I am . . . the One who lives . . . forever and ever" (Revelation 1:18), so that we may in that way become immortal like Him. Jesus is the goal of our lives and nothing less. It is to become one with Him that we have been put on this earth, and so we should not depart from this vision until our objective has been reached—the one of becoming by means of grace all that our Lord Himself is.

THE JOY OF SAINTS

The saints live in a different world from other people. They live and move and are in the kind of world in which everyone will be after this life is over. God gives the saints a living experience of the kind of life He will bring us into after our departure from this world.

The saints encourage us to hope for what cannot be comprehended in the present life. In them we see what we shall ourselves one day be, heavenized human beings, akin to the holy angels. God does not wait for us to die to give us a taste of the joys of the life to come. He gives us these joys in the person of the saints. The saints are the heralds of our future bliss, thus assuring us that we shall one day be unimaginably happy, happy with God's own joy. " . . . in your light we see light," the Psalmist says (Psalm 36:10). He indicates in these words we shall one day be happy in a way in which we cannot now be. "Light" in Hebrew is a metaphor for joy.

All throughout the Scriptures we are assured that we shall one day be inconceivably happy. We must study the Scriptures if we wish to know the kind of happiness awaiting us after we leave this world. It is in Scripture alone that we will find an accurate description of that happiness. To be happy in the life to come, we shall have no need for anything we now need for happiness. We won't need the body itself, at least until the general resurrection, when the body we now have will be restored to the soul in its glorified state. As soon as the soul leaves the body it enters into the kind of joy possessed by God Himself.

The saints have a goodly taste of these joys during the present life. Where would we be without having the saints for an example? How could we endure the troubles of this life without the help they furnish us for such endurance? If there were no saints in the world, we would not want to be in it. We love the saints because we see in them what we should ourselves be. We see in the saints the kind of joy which we ourselves crave, a substantial and intellectual one, the kind that does not have its origin in the present life.

It's not what proceeds from our bodily makeup that makes us happy, but what has its source in our inmost being. It is in vain we seek for happiness outside the Most Holy Trinity. Without the saints to counteract the evils in the world, it would become the "land of darkness and of gloom" of which Job speaks (10:21). Can we picture to ourselves how melancholy this world would be without a Saint Francis of Assisi and a Saint Teresa of Avila to light it up with their own beautiful personalities? It is intolerable to think of such a world, much less wanting to be in it. " . . . We have our citizenship in heaven," Saint Paul says (Philippians 3:20)—the heaven where the saints are.

SAVORING THE DIVINE

"Let me see you" (Song of Songs 2:14).

These words have reference to the supernatural vision of Christ seen substantially in the soul's substance. There is a passage in the "Hebrew and Chaldee Lexicon of Gesenius" which reads as follows: "The Hebrews (like the Greeks and others) not infrequently make use of a verb of *seeing* of those things also which are not perceived by the eyes, but—by other senses, as by hearing; taste, touch, feeling . . . of those things which are perceived, felt, and enjoyed by the mind. Thus it is said to see life, Ecclesiastes 9:0; to see death, Psalm 89:49. Also to see sleep, to see famine, to see good, i.e., to enjoy the good of life, etc." And so when we hear the soul exclaim the above words of the Song of Songs, we should understand them in their deep figurative sense, namely, that of interior and substantial sight of God the Bridegroom, which vision of Him takes place in the soul's substance. In such a way, to see is to enjoy the ineffable Person of Him by whom we have been made and redeemed, and who will constitute our everlasting happiness in the life to come. "Let me see you," the soul says to her divine Lover, and in these words asks for the enjoyment of Him too ineffable for words to express or thought to conceive.

The soul here requests the enjoyment of Jesus had by all the saints during their earthly life.

In the Person of His Son God came to us not merely that we should be able to see Him with the eyes of the body, but that He may in that way become our life, as well as the food and joy of our whole being. God became Man that we might be able to have experience of what He is like. Instead of being content merely to give us something, He wants to share Himself with us. It is for this reason that the Holy Spirit inspires the soul to say to Christ, "Let me see you." In these words the soul asks for the enjoyment of God's divine Son.

We should ask for that sight of God which all the saints have been blessed to receive. Thus seeing Him, the soul will have the courage not to look for anything else to comfort and console it. God is willing to share Himself with us, even in the present life. He has conditioned this sharing of Himself by the desire and holy longing for Him which should be in the heart. " . . . open wide your mouth, and I will fill it" (Ps. 81:11). God wants us to become capable of the vision of Himself possessed by the saints. "Therefore, wait for me," God is saying to us (Zephaniah 3:8). God wants us to be on the lookout for Him and to await His coming in the most perfect way possible, and this even during the present life. He wants us to be engaged in the task of saying to Him, "Come, Lord Jesus!" (Revelation 22:21). It is only by our continual longing for Him that we will be able to enjoy that something ineffable to be had even on this earth.

Looked at from the viewpoint of Christ, things take on another dimension, and we discern in them that by which they are transfigured in Him. "Let me see you, let me hear your voice, for your voice is sweet, and you are lovely" (Song of Songs 2:14). Regarded with reverence, the voice of Christ can be heard in all existing things. Christ the Word can be found in everything, ourselves included. With this realization, we can repeat the words of the Song every minute of the day. We can experience the beauty of Christ in everything around us. Properly viewed, all things become for us a kind of ladder by which God may be reached. "Have you seen Him whom my heart loves? (Song of Songs 3:3), we can say to all things, hinting thereby that He whom our heart loves can be found in all things, seeing they are made by Him.

ONE WITH CHRIST

We can form no more wonderful conception of what the joys of heaven will be like than the one that Jesus is. Our beatitude there will consist in the adoration of the sacred Body of the God-Man and the love we shall be able to have for that Body—the Body which is both divine and human at the same time. If even on earth the contemplation of the Flesh of Christ constitutes such a source of ineffable joy to the soul, what will not the contemplation of that Flesh be for us in all its fullness and perfection?

The sole happiness in this life consists in the contemplation of Christ, and in the love the heart feels every time the thought of Him comes to our mind. For a Christian, there can be no greater delight than the one offered to him by loving the Love itself that Jesus is. However, this delight cannot be fully had in the present life, and so it's for this reason we find it such a trial to be detained in our mortal frames.

"We should like to see Jesus" (John 12:21) is the motto of all the saints. The saints craved a sight of all that our Lord is in His glorified Flesh. We cannot have this sight in the present life in the way we would want to have it, so we wait for the day of our death, by means of which this sight may be attained.

The saints thought of Christ all the time. They thought of Him day and night. No craving that the saints possessed exceeded in ardor and intensity the longing they had for our divine Lord. Jesus was everything to the saints, and anything more wondrously sweet than His divine and human personality they were unable to conceive. The saints were engulfed in the love of Christ. It was the sea of affection in which their souls were drowned.

How intense is the craving of the soul even in this life to become what Jesus Himself is! How overwhelming is the desire of the heart to become an integral portion of our divine Lord! There is only one single longing in the heart and mind of the saints—to become immersed in the divine Good that is Jesus, to love that Good and to become one with It. The longing of the saints is not merely to believe in Christ, but to be what He Himself is. The saint finds it a punishment to live, since to live is to be "away from the Lord" (2 Cor. 5:6) who constitutes his life and his love. For all eternity the delight of the saints will consist in the adoration of the sacred Flesh of the God-Man and to revel in the enjoyment that adoration will bring with it. Jesus is not only God to the saints; He is an ineffable Being for them on whom to expand all the love of their hearts and minds.

It is the desire of the saints not only to become commingled with the sacred humanity of our divine Lord but to become one with that humanity. It is Jesus that the saints wish for both in this life and the next—Jesus, and Him alone. For them, nothing God has made can equal the beauty and goodness that our Lord is. The saints are impervious to everything which God is not—God in the Person of His divine Son. It's this Son of His that they love with all their body and soul.

There is no love like the one we have for Jesus Christ, and so we go on thinking of this day and night. Day and night we keep on thinking how incomparably beautiful Christ is and how that beauty of His extends itself to every part of His divine and human personality. Day and night we think of Jesus Christ and all that He will be for us throughout all eternity. Is there anything else on this earth worth thinking about? Is there anything else that can bring greater joy to the soul than such a thought? We cannot imagine ourselves happier than being with Jesus and being with Him forever and ever. Earth is a lonely place for those who love God, seeing that they cannot be with Him in the way those do who are already in heaven. Earth is indeed the "foreign country" of which the Psalms speak, seeing that all the time we are upon it we are away from the love of our heart that is Jesus.

The saints were Christ-conscious and Christ-minded every moment they lived, and to be as happy as they had been we imitate them in this respect. It's easy to be Christ-conscious and Christ-minded seeing that it's God's will that we should be so all the time we are in this life. "Give us this day our daily bread," we should say to God in this respect. The "daily" food of the soul is our Lord. We must think of Christ in a loving way, so that we may thus become an intimate part of His own sacred Self. Did not our Lord become a human being so that we may in that way become all He Himself is? It is the need of the soul to become completely incorporated into all that our Lord Himself is, so as to in that way attain eternal life.

We have to become what Jesus is or we will never know by personal experience what the joys of heaven are like. Jesus constitutes these joys, and so the more like Him we become, the more perfectly these joys can be had by us. We don't have to wait until we die to know what the joys of heaven are like, since it's God's will we should get a goodly taste of them right here on this earth. We don't have to wait until we die to know by personal experience the beauty of eternity which is beautiful with the beauty of the God-Man. "I love thee, O eternity," Nietzsche said, but little did he realize that without belief in the God-Man, we can form no true conception of what lies beyond the grave.

The word eternity has no meaning without the Holy Name of Jesus coupled with it. Without Christ there can be no thought of the afterlife. Without Him, the grave looms up before the eyes as a dark and dismal thing. We cannot think of heaven unless we do so in connection with the thought of the God-Man. The soul is anxious to leave the body, so as in that way to become what Jesus Himself is. "O how we long for You!" we say to God. We want to return to the home for the soul that is God, and from which home the soul issued forth. "We wish to see Jesus," we say with the disciples of Christ. As long as we live there can be no substitute for such a wish and such a desire. Nothing but Christ can satisfy the soul; hence we crave for a vision of Him in the state of glory. We want not only to "see Jesus" but to become an integral portion of His own Being. We want to become all Jesus Himself is, and as that becoming of Him has been made possible by means of the Incarnation, as the result of God's becoming man, we can now hope one day to be all our Lord Himself is. For all eternity, we want to be another Christ and to experience the delight this transformation of our being into Him will bring with it. Body and soul, we want to become all our Lord Himself is. We want to become divinized in God's divine Son.

We were put on earth to long for the heaven of beauty that is Jesus. We have been born to be coheirs with Jesus Christ—for this, and nothing else. We have been destined for Christ, and it is in this destiny that all our earthly glory lies, and the one in heaven too. We have not been made for an earthly end.

It is for Jesus that we have been born. We have been born so that we may ultimately become what He Himself is and to remain that way for all eternity. We cannot be satisfied with anything less than what God Himself is, and so it's for the sake of the divine that we have to live. God became Man so as to share Himself in that way with us. We love the beauty of the Son of God and worship His sacred Self. Body and soul, we adore all Jesus will be for us through the endless ages of eternity. With this in view, we look forward to our one day being all He Himself is, so that we may in that way love with a love worthy of His ineffable Being. We can only love the love Christ is by ourselves becoming that which we love.

TIME INTO ETERNITY

"Let me see you,
Let me hear your voice,
For your voice is sweet,
And you are lovely."
(Song of Songs 2:14)

In these words the soul asks Christ for a living experience of Himself, and this under the condition of this life. The soul that loves Him is not content to wait until it gets to heaven to see and experience what God is like. It craves a revelation of Him while still in this life. Call this mysticism or what you will. Realizing we have been made in the divine image, we wish to taste what this divine is like right here on earth. Moses asked for such a taste when he asked God to "Let me see your glory" (Exodus 33:18). All the saints have repeated these words with him, though each of them did so in his own way, and in the manner of expression peculiar to him- or herself. They all asked for an embrace of the divine, the divine good that Jesus is. Prior to their departure from this life, they all said, "Come, Lord Jesus" (Revelation 22:20). With these sweet and holy words, the saints left for their home in heaven, there to enjoy to the full all that they loved while here on earth.

Heaven to the saints is not something entirely new, since they all received a goodly taste of the joys that are there all the time they had been in this life. For them, there was no complete break between time and eternity. As far as they were concerned, these two states sort of ran into each other. They were mutually interrelated and intertwined. For the saints, God was the sole Reality, everything else being swallowed up, merged and absorbed in His precious infinitude. Physically the saints lived in time, but spiritually in that somewhere else for which no name can be found. "Let me see You," the saints always say to Christ. With these words before us, we can readily see how fundamentally different was the view the saints had of the divine love of their souls from the rest of the faithful. Loving Christ the way they did, the saints prayed all the time—their love for Him constituting that prayer. "Pray unceasingly," Saint Paul said; all the saints did that very thing. They prayed all the time because their love for things divine never knew any cessation. The majority of the faithful draw a wedge between the profane and the holy, thus making of these two, different spheres of activity. For the saints there was but one world, the one God made which was infused with the grace of the Holy Spirit. Living in uninterrupted communion with the divine, the saints took a completely different attitude towards all things that occurred in time, looking upon them all from a purely supernatural point of view, seeing and detecting God's designs in them.

In everything the saints heard the sweet voice of God and perceived His face, that is to say, His essential presence, the presence that renders all existing things existent. In everything the saints heard the voice of God and perceived the face of His anointed one, Christ the Lord. The saints were thoroughly supernaturalized human beings, and so they perceived that vision in all things undetected by lesser souls. Prayer was the key to the heart of the saints, unlocking for them all secrets and all mysteries, secrets and mysteries connected with their own being as well as with the being of those with whom they were brought into intimate relationship. Everyone loves a saint because we detect in him what is not found in those who are not so dear to God. The saints longed for Christ as they did for nothing else in the whole universe. Longing for Him with the ardor and intensity that they did, they were rendered worthy of the vision of Himself of which the Song of Songs speaks.

As we progress spiritually, heaven becomes the dominant thought of our lives, so that we center all our activities in its direction. "I was not born for this world but for the next,

and so not for this world but for the next I shall live." To
make progress on the road to God, these words of Saint
Stanislaus Kostka, S.J., must become our own. To do so, we
must center our hearts and minds on the kind of life they
already experience who are no longer on this earth. We go to
Jesus in our love for God, and all things we experience here
are nothing but so many stepping stones to the kingdom of
inner riches He came on earth to bring. Creatures become a
kind of ladder on which the soul mounts to those divine
heights on which it is God's will we should always live.

Man is so made that he must have an object in which to
delight himself, and without such an object he cannot live.
To most people, that object is something created by God,
such as friends, a sweetheart, father, mother and so forth.
To the saints, this object of delight is none other than He
from whom all delight proceeds and whom the prophet
designates "the desired of all the nations" (Haggai 2:7,
Vulgate) indicating in these words who and what our delight
should be. Throughout the Scriptures we find Christ referred
to and spoken of in terms which raise our hearts to Himself,
and this on account of the beauty of His being. In the Song of
Songs, this portrayal of Him reaches its most sublime heights,
for He is spoken of in terms that captivate the soul, and
which do not let it find rest save in His own sacred Being.

We cannot properly esteem the beauty of Christ in the
present life, since in order to do so we would have to die.
Perhaps it's for this reason God said to Moses, "for not man
sees me and still lives" (Exodus 33:20). God knew that our
mortal frame would be shattered by the delight such a sight
would cause us, and so He has seen fit to moderate the vision
of Himself in the Person of His divine Son. Christ was the
"hollow of the rock," in which God asked Moses to take
refuge while His glory passed by. In our divine Lord, God
moderates the vision of Himself for our souls to see. In Him,
in Christ, we can see God and still live. "Whoever has seen
me has seen the Father" (John 14:9). In Him the divinity, is
so to speak, shaded by His human nature. Without Christ, we
cannot in this life know what God is like so as to have

personal experience of Him. But in Christ, we can see Him who always is and to whom Moses makes reference in the Book of Exodus. Prior to His coming into the world, it was hard to love God in an intimate and personal way. It was for this reason that the saints of the Old Testament asked for the "kisses" mentioned in the Song of Songs. There is an infinite number of sweet and precious things connected with Christ, and so this Song speaks of them in language that is both sweet and sublime.

A SENSE OF GOD

There is a line in the Psalms that haunts me. According to a free rendition of it in Hebrew, the implication is that if we sanctify ourselves we would as the result of this sanctification receive a vision of the Divine. In other words, to see God we have to have holiness in life—there being no other way of knowing what He is like. It's not easy to see God, for to do so we have to be saints. Why a saint? Because we will thereby be given a vision of things divine. God is everywhere and in everything. We don't have to go to the philosophers to find this out, but to the saints. The saints know God in a way different from those devoid of their own holiness. It's holiness that counts in this respect and no other thing. Do we wish to know what God is like? Do we wish to have an insight into the divine nature? The answer is crystal clear in the words of Psalm 63:3, for it is there said: "Thus have I gazed toward you in the sanctuary to see your power and glory." The Hebrew for "sanctuary" can be translated by "holiness." In holiness we see what God is like and in no other way. This seems to be the impression that line is trying to convey. It is not by reasoning or philosophizing alone that we get an idea of what God is like but by holiness of life. The saints have proven this time and again.

It is to the saints that we have to go to be told how beautiful the things of heaven are. The saints have seen God. They had personal experience of the Divine, and this while still in this life. The saints did not have to wait for death to have received an intimate vision of the Most Holy Trinity. To them, God was the most real thing in the universe; everything in it was a manifestation of Him. They saw God in everything and they did so by the holiness of their lives. We can do the same if we follow in their footsteps and make holiness of life our main goal. The age of wonders has not ceased, but to see them we have, in the words of Saint Paul, to "put on the Lord Jesus Christ" (Romans 13:14). These words mean that we have to clothe ourselves in the divine and live deep supernatural lives, in other words that we try to become saints. Be a saint and you will see God and see Him in everything He has made. There is nothing which, when looked at from the point of view of the supernatural, will not become a source of wonder to us. Thus regarded what is there which will not assume a startling quality and hold us spellbound? The saints were mystics, and so everything with which they came into contact had an entrancing effect on their personality.

How boring many people find everything in this life! How sad it is that they do not know the secrets of the saints in this respect? If they did, the things they looked at would undergo a kind of transfiguration before their eyes. They would behold in these things that which God intended to be seen. Have we ever reflected on the fact of what a marvelous thing our own being is? How astonished we would be at ourselves if we were holy as the saints! All things are full of mystery, of marvel and wonder. The reason that we do not perceive it is the lack of sanctity in our lives. Sanctity enables us to see that which would otherwise be hidden from our view. God is seen by the saints in a way more intimately than that of other people. The reason for this is their sanctity. Moses saw God "face to face." He beheld God without any intermediary. The same thing is true of Saint Paul and others who have been equally holy. We don't have to wait for death to see God. We can do this while still in the flesh.

There are a lot of people who are devoid of the sense of the supernatural, and so it is vain to talk to them of what is so clear to those who are endowed with this sense. Unless our lives are holy it is in vain that we will reach out for the heights of heaven. There is a complete blackout in some people as far as the things of heaven are concerned, for they know not what sanctity is. We have been told that the pure of heart shall see God. But what is purity of heart but sanctity and holiness? The saints see God directly and without any intervening medium. The saints see Him face to face, which simply means that they have an experience of the divine in an intimate and personal way.

In the above words of the Psalmist, we are told that we shall see God if we are holy. It is not philosophy or science that merits such a vision but holiness of life. We have to "believe," Isaiah says, in order to "understand," and we cannot believe unless our hearts are free from impurities of every kind. It is to the single-minded and single-hearted that God reveals His intimate secrets and gives them a vision of Himself that renders them beside themselves with joy. To know God in a personal way, only one thing is necessary— holiness of life. Possessing this holiness endows the soul with a capacity for the divine. Without holiness, this capacity cannot be had. The saints were men and women who had in themselves a capacity for the divine. It was this that constituted their essential characteristic.

THE NATURE OF PRAYER

The best way to learn how to pray is to have a continual longing for heaven and to realize how insubstantial and how fragile all things in this life are. We pray badly because we settle down in this life as if it were our true and real home. We don't live in it as strangers but as residents. The saints never felt themselves at home in this life, but in that somewhere else where our Lord is. To pray well is to be detached in heart and mind and look forward to the day when we shall arrive in our home in heaven. This life is a stopover place on our way to what is infinitely better than anything to be had in it. When we realize the truth of this, we pray well. Prayer consists in the realization that we have been made for infinitely better things than those to be had in our mortal state. It consists in a longing for heaven. The more ardent and sincere this longing is, the better we pray.

Prayer consists in the proper evaluation of the things of the present life, so that we do not overemphasize their importance, but keep them in the bounds intended by God. We are going to die one day, and so this thought should continually be in our heart. It should determine our actions and pursuits. When the thought of our departure from this life is missing or weak, our whole view of existence becomes false and we are victims of deceit. To pray well we have to reflect constantly on the truths of our faith, the truth, especially, that life on this earth is a shadowy thing. "Man is like a breath," the Psalmist tell us (Psalm 144:4). He reminds us in these words how we should feel and think all the time we find ourselves away from our true home in the life to come. We pray well when we live well, and we cannot live well without the practice of the Christian virtues. There is no easy way of learning how to pray well, because there is no easy way of learning how to live the kind of life laid down in the Gospel teachings.

Someone once said to Saint Ignatius Loyola about another: "There goes a man of great prayer." The saint countered these words with the reply: "There goes a man of great mortification." Prayer consists in carrying the Cross by the acceptance of whatever it is God's will for us to endure. The promptness with which this is done determines the value of our prayer. God looks at the heart, and it's there our prayer is made. We don't have to worry too much about our exterior posture when we pray. The important thing is to yield up our whole being to God. Do we live for the things of the next life or the ones to be had in time? It is by means of such thoughts that we can find out whether we pray well.

It can be seen from this that the subject of prayer is not simple, and that it involves the way and manner in which we conduct ourselves in this life.

> "Happy the man who follows not the counsel of the wicked
> Nor walks in the way of sinners, nor sits in the company of the insolent,
> But delights in the law of the Lord and meditates on his law day and night."   (Ps. 1:1-3)

From these words we get a pretty good idea of what the condition for prayer should be, and that a man prays the way he lives. "Do you want to pray well?" God says to us in these words. "Then live in accordance with the teachings of My divine Son."

One of the most important things to be remembered in connection with prayer is that it is an exercise not limited to the time when we are in Church, and that it is something perpetual with us. We can pray all the time and in all circumstances, there not being a minute in our life in which we cannot be given over to the admiration of all of God's works and become absorbed in the wonder of them. We can pray all the time by loving God in everything He has made, ourselves included. We are a great mystery to ourselves, and so all we have to do to pray is to reflect on the mystery of our own being. We can pray all the time since not a minute exists in which we cannot detect the divine in all existing things. Everything we see, hear, taste and touch can become for us an object for prayer. There can be no limit to the different ways we can communicate with God in this life. They are as numerous as our thoughts and feelings.

How vast are the inner experiences we undergo in this life! How numerous the ways in which we are able to be reminded of God and of our ultimate destiny! Every time we think of ourselves in connection with Christ and with our neighbor, we pray. Every time we look at anything God has made, we can make that thing a means by which to lift up our hearts and minds to Him. There are no limits to how this can be done. They are as numerous as existing things. As we go on living a life in union with Christ, the knowledge of prayer will grow with us. Every day that goes by, we can become more proficient in this science and in this art, and what science or art is more wonderful than the one prayer is? What can bring us a greater amount of happiness than learning how to pray? Without prayer nothing worthwhile can be achieved in this life, at least as far as the things of heaven are concerned. It is by prayer that the door to heaven is opened.

THE MEANING OF SUFFERING

Suffering detaches us from the accidental things of this life so that thus detached we may get the grace to cling and cleave to what is permanent and essential in it. To put it in the words of the golden-mouthed Doctor of the Church, St. John Chrysostom, "suffering destroys in us the sympathy we have for the present life." To dispose ourselves for the grace of detachment, it is not enough to read spiritual books and to meditate on things eternal—we must suffer, and this in both body and mind.

Many in the Church would become the saints it is God's will they should be if only they would pray for the grace to accept suffering in the right Christian way. Long ago the Apostle to the Gentiles told those around him that it is not enough to perform the various deeds and acts usually effected by those who love Christ; he laid down as an indisputable principle that they must also partake of the Cross of Christ if they would hope to share in the glory of His risen state.

Many years back I asked my venerated and learned spiritual director, what is the purpose of suffering in the life of a Christian? He answered me in these unforgettable words: "Suffering serves to remove the impediments between the soul and God." The problem of Christian pain and Christian mortification is not emphasized today, and it is this lack of emphasis that is responsible for so much of the pseudo-spirituality of our times. To know what God is like we have to suffer, since without suffering we can never have a living experience of all that He Is in His Essential Self.

We cannot know Christ unless we suffer, since it is by means of the Cross that He can be recognized, felt and believed in. We cannot know what the divine sweetness of God is like unless we ask for the grace to bear whatever we have to in the right Christian way. There is a liturgy of the Cross, and if this is neglected our whole conception of the Church has to undergo revision.

Did not St. Paul say, "I would speak of nothing but Jesus Christ and him crucified"? According to these words, to run away from the Cross is to run away from Christ and all the beautiful things promised to us as the result of His becoming Man, such as the resurrection from the dead and the enjoyment of everlasting happiness after this brief and painful existence has come to an end. We cannot love Christ save in the way He has Himself indicated we should love Him, and that way is the way of the Cross.

There is so much false spirituality in the world today that one has to be careful not to become victimized by the many false ideas the enemy of the human race has let loose in the world. The devil does not want us to be happy in this life nor at peace in it, and so it is for this reason he raises up heretics to corrupt the purity of our God-given faith. He it was who put an end to the paradisal bliss enjoyed by our first parents before they sinned, and he it is who does all he can to sow seeds in our minds and hearts as regards all God would have us believe in, hope for, and cherish. However, if we accept suffering in the right Christian way, this acceptance of it will serve to neutralize the satanic influences the enemy of mankind will try to insinuate into our soul, and we will thus be immunized against all of his designs.

It may be asked, why do so many religious leave the Church today? The answer to this question may be much simpler than it seems: The fact that those who leave the Church and desert their God-given vocation to the priestly and religious life have ceased to ask God for the grace to bear whatever they have to in the right Christian way, and so they become victims of a hope for illusory happiness that will never materialize. Running away from the Cross is directly responsible for the many defections in the Church of Christ even as it has been responsible for such defections in the times gone by. The unalterable truth will always be that we cannot be happy in this life nor at peace in it without the

Cross, so that to reject the Cross is to reject the only kind of happiness possible for a Christian to have this side of heaven.

"If we suffer with Christ, we shall also rejoice with Him." It is in these words that the solution to all our earthly problems lies; they do so in no other way, in no other plan of life and in no other scheme of existence devised by those who are ignorant of the plan for the well-being, the peace and happiness God has from all eternity decreed for the human race. What a lot of heartaches could be avoided, and what a large amount of useless pain if only we asked for the grace to know the purpose for which an infinitely loving and good God put us on this earth.

We are here for no other end than doing God's holy will, since if this is accomplished we will have no other problems with which to cope. And what is this will of God? It is to embrace in our own lives what the Savior of the world embraced and suffered all the time He was on this earth. It is in this imitation of Christ that God's holy will is achieved and accomplished by us.

"I see many crucified people," a saint said, "but I see few who are crucified by the Cross of Christ." How fundamentally true these words of Saint John Eudes will always be! So many people suffer in this life, but what they go through is of no avail to them as regards the peace and happiness they are meant by God to have as the very result and consequences of these sufferings of theirs.

Without Christ the sufferings men go through have no meaning whatsoever and are even injurious to the higher part of our being; sometimes, nay, often, they seem to poison and embitter that in ourselves which was meant by God to be sweet, benign and cheerful. Without Christ pain is wasted and ends up in all sorts of tragic consequences, such as suicide and unbelief. Without Christ all we have to suffer in this life acts as a kind of pall on the soul, casting a dark shadow on everything we do and are. Without Him we live and suffer in vain. Without Him our whole existence ends up in the kind of vanity, delusion and futility mentioned in the Book of Qoheleth or Ecclesiastes, in which we are told that "all is vanity and vexation of the flesh."

WORLD TO COME

In this life, the body has to disintegrate so that it may be fashioned anew in Christ at the resurrection of the dead. "Charity," Saint Francis de Sales says, "obliges us to love our bodies as befits them as essential to our good deeds, as part of ourselves, as due to share in eternal bliss."

It is wonderful to love our friends in Christ, for they are transfigured in Him, and it is also wonderful to love our bodies for the above-mentioned reason. In the life to come, our bodies will be a source of joy to us, and we will never be able to thank God enough for having given them to us. After the Resurrection, the body will have a uniqueness about it which we cannot now imagine—substantially, it will be the same body that we now have, only it will be completely transfigured in Christ.

We should rejoice at the thought of death because it means going home to God. God will give us a new body after we get rid of the one we now possess. Its newness will consist in being freed from its present defects and being perfected in a divine manner. God allows the body we now have to disintegrate because He has in view the kind we shall one day have in heaven.

Old age is nothing in the eyes of God because He sees the eternal youth which will one day be ours. Sickness and disease concern Him not because He knows that what we now call health is itself a kind of sickness, and life, death.

At present, if we stop eating, we die, but in the life to come, Christ will be the only food we will then need. We should not worry about the so-called evils of the present life, since they are only a temporary phase of our existence in Him who always is. The real life comes after we leave this world.

We must love ourselves in Christ and love all others in Him. Outside of Christ nothing is worth having; outside of Him all is sham and a hollow mockery. Apart from Christ this life is only a bad dream, and without faith in Him, we are mere phantoms. The shadows will flee away after this life is over and give way to what is genuine and true.

We cannot hold on to anything because time is always taking it out of our hands. It robs us of everything except Christ Himself. He alone will remain at the end of our journey through this world which has to end up at the foot of the grave. It is with this in view that the Prophet says: "Where are your plagues, O death! Where is your sting, O nether world!" (Hosea 13:14).

We have to have recourse to Christ or we are dead men and women—dead to the only thing worthwhile having which is summed up in His Divine Person. The devil tries to depress us by separating us from the truths of faith. There is nothing he hates so much as our belief in the life to come. The devil cannot have that life and so he does all he can to insinuate that it's only an illusion of the mind.

However, Christ came to destroy the works of the devil, chief among which are those of unbelief. The devil hates Christians in a particular way; he berates them for believing all that God has revealed concerning His Divine Son. The devil's main attack is on the truths of our holy faith. He hates eternity and does all he can to uproot the love of it from the hearts of men.

We can defeat the wiles of Satan by living a life in conformity with God's holy will. It is good to ponder on all that our Lord has procured for us by His Sacred Passion and Death. Do we repay Him for this by our having an ardent desire for the life to come? The saints were anxious to die; the desire for heaven inflamed their hearts, and so why should we not follow their own example? With Saint Paul they all cried out, "I long to be dissolved and to be with Christ."

We should long for heaven, the saints tell us, for it's the only thing worth wishing for in this life. "On my bed, I sought him whom my heart loves—I sought him but I did not find him" (Song of Songs 3:1).

We cannot find God in this life in the way we would like to have Him, and so we look forward to being with Him in the life to come. The bodies we now have are a source of misery to us and so we think of the time when we shall be rid of them. Death is a merciful release from the ills of this life, and so we should think of this with our whole heart.

What a wonderful thing it is to have faith, there being no substitute for belief in Christ. Can anyone else but Christ provide us with the comfort He alone is able to bestow?

"I rejoiced because they said to me, we shall go up to the house of the Lord" (Ps. 122:1). The Psalmist had his own death in view when he wrote these words, and if we were wise we would think of them in connection with our own departure from this life. Death has no terrors for those who love God but only for those who do not love Him.

THE MYSTERY OF MAN

When we look at a human being we perceive something divine; we cannot get rid of God, for every human being bears the image of Him in himself. How foolish the atheist is, since his own existence gives the lie to his particular philosophy.

God speaks to us from out of the soul of every living person with whom we are brought into intimate relationship, since that person speaks to us with the gift of speech he has received from God. There is not anyone in whom the divine does not dwell and in whom the trace of the Deity cannot be found. Men look at us from out of the eyes they have received from God. How fascinating are the souls of men, since it is in these souls that God dwells!

God is not somewhere far off; He is right here within ourselves. In heaven we will see that the Divine was never far off, though in our blindness we were convinced that He was. Where can God be found? The answer is clear and distinct: He exists within ourselves; He lives in that part of our being that raises us above the rest of creation.

God lives in every existing human being; every human being is a theological proof of the existence of God. God makes use of the mind and heart of man through whom He makes Himself evident. Even a sinner has God in himself, and that is why both the Lord and all His saints loved Him so much.

Sometimes the image of the Deity is obscured in those whose lives are ones of sin, but it is never completely obliterated. We find proofs of the existence of God in every human being we meet, for He exists in them all. Everyone born of woman carries something in himself he cannot completely comprehend. There is something infinite in man and that's the reason for his being so deeply perplexed.

The forces of evil are bent on uprooting the divine to be found in every human being that lives. These forces cannot understand the mystery of the Godhead in that person. Christ is always around; He makes Himself evident by the gifts with which we have all been endowed. When will we get the grace to realize by personal experience that God is not far off, but right here within ourselves?

The image of Him has been implanted in our souls, and so, try as we may, we will never succeed in ridding ourselves of something divine, that something divine without which we could not be the men and women we are. A human being is sacred.

At the end of our earthly pilgrimage God will come to take us to Himself, and we will then see how profoundly mysterious everything is.

By means of the Incarnation, God has made a contract with us, so that we cannot leave Him even if we would. "You have the words of eternal life," we say to Jesus, and so where else can we go for that life? (John 6:69). All things are shrouded in ineffable mystery including our own lives. We live, and this life of ours is the proof that God exists. We shall never get rid of the mystery of this life, and so it is this mystery that keeps God in the world.

Looked at with the eyes of faith, everything we see becomes a source of wonder to us, and try as we may, we cannot completely eradicate it from our lives, and this no matter how humdrum these lives of ours become. There will always be a startling element in connection with ourselves, and it is of this stuff that poetry is made. There would be no poets if there were no mystery in the world. Aristotle would never have been what he became were it not for the fact that there is something very startling about every existing thing.

Christ came to point out how wonderful and mysterious all things are. He came to lead us to Himself by arousing in us the sense of wonder. The Jews of old fell away from the truth because they ceased to wonder at all things wonderful. We die spiritually when we cease to look at ourselves in a wonderful and startling way.

The divine is in everything, and it only remains for us to ask for the grace to be able to take cognizance thereof. How strangely mysterious life is, and death too! Can we not see something divine looking at ourselves through the eyes of another person?

It's all so mysterious and fascinating, this entering into intimate relationship with another human being like ourselves, for God is present when two people meet and exchange glances with one another. What and who is it that looks at us from the eyes of men? Is it not something divine, making use of the senses by which to carry on that kind of communication?

There will be friendships in heaven, but friendship has to start on this earth. We have to permit ourselves to become fascinated by every existing thing, for it is only in this way we will get to know what the divine is like, and knowing that divinity, we shall come to love it. There are a lot of bored people in the world, and this is due to the fact that they do not permit themselves to become swallowed up in the mystery of their being.

Mystery is everything, and in it we find God. God is a very mysterious Being, and so He has shrouded all things in His own nature. He wants us to be fascinated by the world, and so He does not permit it to be completely understood. Mystery is the key to the universe and in it we live, move and have our being.

Do we make an effort to carry out the injunction of Christ not to cease wondering at all existing things, ourselves included? We shall never be able to know ourselves until we are safe in heaven, for it is there alone we shall completely understand.

Man is nothing, the Scriptures tell us, but at the same time, the writers never tire of pointing out the infinite value they have in Christ. We cannot understand ourselves without Christ; neither can we have any kind of existence apart from Him. We are Christians, and this means that we are rooted in the Divine Being of our Lord. We have nothing in ourselves which is not completely His, for, body and soul, we are His property. He it is who keeps us in existence, even in a physical way.

We live in Christ and in the mystery of His Being. The Psalmist was fascinated every time he reflected as to who and what he was: "I give you thanks," he says to God, "that I am fearfully, wonderfully made" (Psalm 139:14).

THE BEAUTY OF MAN

We are mysteries, and in this life we shall never be anything else. In heaven alone will be erased the question as to who and what we are. "Desolate all the land, because no one takes it to heart" (Jerem. 12:11), that is, the mystery of his existence. We don't reflect enough upon ourselves, and that is why our minds are so unproductive; or, if we do reflect, we fail to do so in the right Christian way, and look upon ourselves as God would have us do, namely, as living images of God's divine Son, in and through whom we have been brought into being.

It is only when we look upon ourselves in Christ, as in a mirror, that we will be able to perceive the wonderfulness of our being and the riches of our nature, redeemed as that nature has been by Him. To see ourselves as we truly are, we have to look at ourselves in Christ. It is in the direct proportion that we will marvel at Him that we will be given the grace to be able to wonder at the wonderfulness of our own being, as well as to receive the joy and consolation to be derived from such holy wonderment.

Our lives become devoid of significance unless, by means of contemplation, we descent into the depths of our own being and perceive the wonder that's there.

"Out of the depths I cry to you," the Psalmist says to God (Ps. 130). We should say the same things to Him every time we get the grace to perceive what an impenetrable mystery we are to ourselves and how we shall never be able to probe into the full extent thereof during this present life.

By means of prayer we call out to God and make known to Him all that with which our hearts are so full. We ask for the grace to make us known to ourselves, and to be revealed in God's divine Son. It is in Him alone that we can be fully known to ourselves, and in a way in which we cannot now comprehend. There is a nearness to God in a human being to be found in nothing else the universe contains, and this is proven by the fact that St. Paul says: "Perhaps you do not realize that Christ Jesus is in you" (2Cor.13:5).

Man is a mystery, and if we reflect on this we will come to realize that these two words (man and mystery) are coincidental, for there is a relationship between God and ourselves which does not exist in anything else He has made.

We have but to study the spiritual makeup of a human being in order to realize that he is a living image of the Deity, and Christ came to redeem us on account of the similarity which exists between Him and ourselves, so that to find God in the concrete we have but to study our own nature in a holy and prayerful way.

There is a reverence for man lacking in the world today, and it's due to the fact that we fail to realize how sacred in the eyes of God our immortal souls are, and the body too, on account of its resurrectibility.

We shall one day live forever the kind of life shared by the holy angels, and it is this consideration we should bring to bear every time we look at a human being. We should bear in mind that we are looking at an ineffable mystery in the form of flesh with blood: if we do this, we will find everything in the universe startling to us.

We need more fascination in our lives and it can only be had by contemplating Christ. We have to center our hearts and minds on Him alone and disregard everything else He is not. We have to reflect on Christ and the human nature He has assumed out of love—as the result of the Incarnation man and God are ineffably united, and this with a mode of union that will last forever.

Our human nature is included in this union and that is why it should be sacred to us. We should look upon man as a reflection of the divine, for it is only then we get the grace to contemplate man in the proper Christian way. We cannot be divorced from God by whom we have both been made and redeemed.

We should let ourselves become ecstatic about Christ and enraptured by the beauty of His Being. St. John of the Cross speaks about this enrapturement when he says: "Let us act . . . that we may come to set ourselves in Thy beauty: that is, that we may be alike in beauty, and that Thy beauty may be such that, when one of us looks at the other, each may be alike to Thee in Thy beauty" (Spiritual Canticle, Stanza 35).

PRAYER: A PATH TO GOD

When we look into ourselves we see a depth we cannot fathom. We see God who is the innerness in ourselves. He is the kingdom of heaven to which Christ refers. We cannot comprehend what God is because He is incomprehensible. But when we pray we feel Him present in ourselves in a way impossible for us to describe.

We don't know how God is united to us and we to Him, but when we pray an intercourse takes place between the creature and the Creator. There is something in us that does not belong to time, and when we pray we are brought into contact with an order of experience the senses of the body are unable to reach.

Prayer is the effort the soul makes to establish relationship with its naked essence, with that part of ourselves which will always remain incomprehensible to the mind and hidden from the view of those who have no faith in the existence of the supernatural. There is something in us only faith can come to know—ourselves as we exist in God and not outside of Him.

For just as trees are rooted in the earth, so is there something in us ourselves centered in God which cannot be seen save by those whose hearts have been purified by faith in Christ: our innermost as is contrasted by our outward selves, which is made manifest to those who pray and to them alone.

When we pray we come into contact with that part of ourselves which will always exist and which the poet Goethe called "a piece of eternity." How many there are who live lives in total ignorance of their own being and who go down to the grave unknown to themselves.

There are spiritual tragedies that are far worse than physical ones. They affect men and women who never know who they really are and who never see in themselves that something divine made in the image and likeness of God.

When we pray we turn our eyes inward to find what the outward world cannot have—immortality, for what the eyes can see will pass away with time, not having in itself that substantial nature to last forever. "We do not fix our gaze on what is seen," St. Paul tells us, "but on what is not seen. What is seen is transitory; what is not seen lasts forever" (2 Cor. 4:18).

In these words are summed up what should be the philosophy of every Christian man and woman, that of innerness contrasted with outwardness, substance and not accident. We should concern ourselves with the real and not with the apparent, for the real is seen with the eyes of the soul, whereas the apparent is seen with those of the body.

When we pray we see things that are not disclosed to the view of our bodily sight and which transcend the worth of all outward goods. The saints looked within and not without, and that's why they became holy, for innerness sanctifies while external things distract from God.

The eternal exists for the sake of the internal and is a means thereto. The contemplation of what's outward leads to the reflection on inward beauty that cannot be expressed in shape and form.

We need the arts to stir up in ourselves the longing for a beauty that cannot be described and is seen in the substance of the soul. We need the perishable only for the purpose of bringing us to the imperishable. For just as night leads to day and dusk to dawn, so does the temporal lead to the eternal, and the finite to the infinite.

We must seek in ourselves for what can never have an end with time, and we do this every time we pray and ask God to reveal Himself to the eyes of our soul. We see God every time we peer into ourselves for He is present in the substance of our soul.

The saints were men and women who made innerness the main object of their lives, for they lived buried in the depths of their own being. "Contemplation," St. Gregory the Great tells us, "is a grave in which the soul is buried," and so those who practice prayer are really dead and cut off from the world in the same way as those who are no longer physically in it.

Prayer enables us to descend into the depths of our being as into a kind of ocean that has no bounds in time and is fathomless. By means of prayer the soul plunges into the sea of the endlessness that God is, and refreshes itself with the waters of His grace.

By means of prayer the soul is cleansed from sin in the same way as water washes away the stains from the clothing we wear. We have to bathe our soul in the same way as we do our body, and we do this every time we pray and every time we penetrate into ourselves, for that is what prayer is.

Prayer is an entering into ourselves in the same way as we go into a house. We are the house God built with stone made in heaven. The substance of our soul is the mystical home in which God has taken up His abode, and so let us, out of love and regard for Him, visit Him there.

We have to pray for the grace to be able to enter into ourselves so as to find what can be had nowhere else—Christ and the infinite riches of His Being. We must find God in ourselves or we will find Him nowhere else.

God exists in ourselves, and so we can find Him there if we take time out to pray, for by means of prayer we can find God in the depths of our being, and thus found, we have the infinite.

OPENING THE DOOR

In the words of Scripture Christ beseeches the soul to open itself to the influences of His grace so that He may in that way beautify it with His divine beauty. The infinite beauty of His own Being knocks in a kind of rivalry with the beauty we find in created things. By means of the created beauty around us, Christ knocks at the door of our soul, telling us that we should love Him who is the author and creator of this beauty.

"It was Your beauty," Saint Augustine said to God, "that drew me to You. Heaven and earth were shouting to me from all sides that I must love You" (Confessions). In the expression "heaven and earth" are included all the things that God has made, both visible and invisible realities, those of mind and body, sensible and insensible good things, those we enjoy in a physical way as well as those we can only comprehend with the powers of our mind and which same are a delight to contemplate.

By means of all these things, God knocks at the door of our hearts and minds and tells us that we should love Him. All created good things have been brought into being—ourselves included. We, too, constitute part of the good things God has made, by means of which He wishes we should rise to a love of His own divine Self.

There are ten thousand ways in which God is calling us every moment of the day, in beseeching and imploring us by these ways for the love of our whole hearts and our whole minds, so He may thus suffuse them with Himself in the Person of His divine Son. "Come to me all you that labor and are heavy laden and I will give you rest." This "rest" is often interpreted to mean the highest kind of delight to be found in this life, which same can only be had in Him Who is Delight in Essence and Nature. It was this kind of delight to be found only in Christ, that Job speaks about when, in reference to those whose lives are evil, he says: "Will he then delight in the Almighty?" (Job 27:10).

Creatures are continually knocking at the door of our heart imploring for our love. They do so by means of the beauty with which they have been endowed by God, so that there is in this way a kind of rivalry between the beauty that God has made and the one to be had in His own infinite Being. Temporal and eternal beauty are constantly clamoring at our hearts for the whole love that's in these hearts, and our salvation depends on the decision we make in reference to these two different kinds of beauty.

"My son, give me your heart," Our Lord says to us in the Book of Proverbs (23:26). By "heart," is meant a person's very self, or the essence of all that he is, that part of himself made in the image of God which will go on existing for all eternity. It is this God, this Lord, this Christ, who is knocking at the door of our heart, and He does so in a kind of rivalry to the beautiful things which have been made by Him, and which same were meant to be a kind of road and pathway to Himself. Creatures are good in that they lead to the Creator. Without this end in view, namely, the one Christ is, that which is good is turned into evil, since it fails to fulfill the purpose for which it has been brought into being—that of leading us to Him by whose bounty it exists.

The saints never tire of saying to us that when we look at a beautiful thing we should think of Him by whom this beautiful thing has been made, thus making the sight of it a kind of prayer, a prayer of thanksgiving to God for the creation thereof. The saints became what they were by looking at beautiful things so that by the sight of them their minds and hearts could be raised up to the contemplation of the Deity.

There comes a time in everyone's life when he has to make a choice, an infinite or finite good, and it is on this choice that a person's eternity depends. There comes a time when he either opens or closes the door of his heart to the knocking that's made upon it by Him Who is Love in essence and nature. If he opens that door he is saved, otherwise he is lost to the kind of happiness waiting for him as soon as he closes his eyes in death.

"Here I stand knocking at the door; if anyone hears me calling and opens the door, I will enter his home and eat with him, and he with me," Our Lord says to each one of us (Rev. 3:20).

Our free will is the key to the door our heart is, and with it we can keep the love Christ is out or in. As was said before, there are ten thousand ways by which He who loves us stands at the door of our hearts, beseeching and pleading to accept the many graces He has to offer at each moment of the twenty-four-hour day, and by means of everything He either directly wills or permits to happen to us. Someone said that "God is a sea of honey," and so it is by means of the sweetness of His Being He leads us to Himself.

WHAT THE HEART SEEKS

The flesh of Christ is a vehicle upon which we are borne to heaven, and we can get there in no other way than by means of our devotion to that Flesh. In eternity the blessed contemplation thereof shall constitute our bliss.

In Christ God became Man to draw near to us. And so we revere His Fresh by means of which this was done. We cannot get to know what God is like except through Christ, who is His divine Son. What a wonderful grace to be able to love the Sacred Humanity of our divine Lord and what a misfortune not to know this Humanity by personal experience! The mystics were united to God in a way unknown but to themselves alone—they were unable to communicate to others what they felt in the substance of their soul. Christ was real to the saints; He alone constituted their All so they had no other form of love. Christ was their Beloved One, the Bridegroom mentioned so often in the Song of Songs.

This Lover and Bridegroom was different from all other lovers and so the bliss they derived from being intimately united with Him transcended all earthly joys. The saints had a special devotion to the Sacred Humanity of our Lord and revered His Flesh as belonging to the God-Man. When we look at a picture of our Lord, we try to increase in ourselves a love for the mystery of the Incarnation.

Why should God have become Man? We shall only fully know this when we are face-to-face with His divine Son in paradise. On earth, the reason for this is shrouded in mystery—something of this great mystery we may understand when we read the lives of the saints, especially the great mystics like St. Teresa of Avila.

God gave these saints a personal experience of the beauty of His Being, so that they could actually feel Him substantially in the substance of their soul. The saints could never

tire of contemplating the beauty of Christ. Day and night
they longed for the time when they would enjoy that beauty
in all its fullness in the state of glory.

For the saints there was nothing more beautiful than the
beauty of Christ; they loved to contemplate His Sacred
Humanity and revel in the joy such contemplation brought
with it. What can be more rewarding than to think of Christ
day and night? It was this meditation on the beauty of the
Son of God that the Psalmist had in mind when he said that
he delighted "in the law of the Lord," and meditated "on his
law day and night" (Ps. 1:2). The "Sweet Singer of Israel"
had our Lord in view when he wrote this psalm. We should
think of this when we recite its words so that we may enjoy
their true meaning more fully.

How wonderful to be able to love God made Man! What a
grace it is to be able to contemplate the Flesh of Christ and to
feel oneself drawn close to that Flesh in a mystical way! God
loved us so much that He actually became one of us. He took
Flesh so as to be near to us and share our own experiences.
We should think of this every time we look at an image of
Christ. We should think of the beauty of His Being so as to
long to become immersed in that beauty. We should want to
be made beautiful with the beauty of Christ—this is the only
reason for being Catholics. We are Catholics so that we can
share in the intimate experiences of the Son of God. We have
been born to love God that by so doing we may be made one
with that Love.

Words fail when we try to speak of all that our Lord is, and
it is right that this should be so. Who can talk adequately of
God? Who can express His divine attributes? Who can
penetrate into the mystery of His love in the form of the
Incarnation? Is it any wonder those who love Him should
long to be with Him in a way in which death alone can make
possible?

The saints had a special devotion to the Sacred Heart, and
so they could never tire of having this Humanity before their
minds' eye. Day and night they dwelt on the beauty of
Christ's Being; day and night they speculated on the kind of

joy which shall be theirs as soon as this life is over. Shall we not do what the saints have done? Shall we not think of Christ day and night and make the meditation of the beauty of His Being our sole earthly occupation?

Why can't we do all that the saints have done, that is, think of Christ all the time? Who is there to prevent us from imitating their example? Who is more worthwhile to think about than Christ? Whose Being is more wonderful to contemplate? What greater joy than to love the Flesh of Christ and to long to become co-mingled with that Flesh?

"My lover belongs to me and I to him" (Song of Songs 2:16). These words come to us from the Holy Spirit and have reference to the transformation of the soul in God. They encourage us to become what He Himself is. Our happiness on earth consists in longing for Christ.

No experience we can have in this life can be as satisfying as the one that comes with being with Christ. Nothing created can afford us the pleasure we derive from being close to Christ. Nothing can so transform us into angels as this experience. We have been made for the divine, which has been made available to us by the Flesh of Christ.

What a grace it is to be a Christian, for being a Christian is to be Christ's! To be a Christian is to be His in the most intimate way possible in this life—it is this which distinguishes Christianity from all other religions, for Christianity is Christ—it is God made Man and so rendered accessible to mortal creatures. We cannot ascend into heaven, and so God has descended to us. He became Man to be with us in the most intimate way possible. We should think of this day and night, for the joy that such a thought brings along with it is inestimable.

The majority of men have always believed that if they had this or that they would be happy. It is with this in view they labor so much to make this world the kind of place they think it should be in order to have this happiness. The majority of mankind will always fail to realize that it's Christ they really long for and that it's Him they have to have in order to be the happy people they feel they should become.

They fail to realize Christ alone is able to fulfill the desire within ourselves for that something for which no other name can be found—that something which Christ alone is. They fail to realize that being born to love, they have to find the proper object on which this love can be centered. The world, too, holds out to us objects on which to center the love of our hearts. The world tries to compete with Christ but is defeated in this attempt—what the world has to offer has to be left standing at the foot of the grave.

From time immemorial men have searched for something, they knew not what, and so they called it by different names. Plato named this something by one name and another by another. The time came when this something which men always craved appeared on earth and took our human nature, so that we may know what it was we craved so much.

How glowingly the Sacred Scriptures speak of the beauty of Christ and in what sweet and sublime accents! We have but to turn to the words of the Song of Songs to know that this is so. Both in this Song and the Psalms of David it is Christ alone who is spoken of and in imagery sweet to contemplate. We cannot do without Christ any more than we can do without love, He being but another word for that love. We have been made for love and so we cannot rest until we have by means of grace become that which we love.

ONE WITH CHRIST

Take away the Church and some people could no longer go on living. Without faith in her, they would be devoid of strength and help. For some people faith and life are inseparable. Such people say: "For, to me, 'life' means Christ; hence dying so much gain" (Philip. 1:21). They equate their existence with their holy Catholic religion, and so they cannot conceive of them as being apart from one another.

Like all the saints, they know only one kind of life and it's the one led by our Lord when He was on earth. It's He they follow, imitate and emulate. They live by His doctrines and feel as He did. Such people cannot think of themselves apart from Christ and the Church which he founded, so completely have they become suffused with the blessed Being of the Son of God. "My lover belongs to me and I to him," they say in the words of the Song of Songs. Nothing such people do is performed without reference to Him who is the Way, the Truth and the Life, for they always have the divine Exemplar before their mind's eye and look into the mirror of perfection He alone is.

The Church is everything to us, for without her everything anyone can have in this life is not worth possessing. Take away the Church and the world becomes the same dark and gloomy place it had been prior to the coming of Christ into the world. How depressing to read the plays of Sophocles or Euripedes or any other of the ancient Greek tragedies! How dark and despairing are the thoughts they contain! In contrast with these, how bright and cheerful are the Gospels of Christ, or the Psalms of David, or any other portions of the Sacred Scripture. In the latter there is joy; in the former there is a dread that chills the heart and fills it with misgiving of every kind and dark foreboding.

"I am the light of the world," our Lord said, and to the Semitic mentality "light" is synonymous with "joy." The Psalms are full of joy; they are replete with delight of every kind, and this job, this delight, diffuses itself in the Church. It's a delight to be a Catholic and a holy ecstasy of love to be a member of the household of God that the Church will always be. She is the heavenly Jerusalem coming down to us from above and the mystical city envisioned by the prophets of old. In her is to be had the life everlasting our Lord came to bring—the life everlasting we shall live forever after we die. The Church is all this and infinitely more—she is all this because through her all this is obtained.

The Church is vast and limitless. She existed before time was, and she will continue to be after this world is no more. How many Caesars has she not outlived! She has been present at the funerals of those whose task it was to bring about her destruction. She is the kingdom of Christ, and therefore divine as is He Himself. The Prophet Daniel writes of her when he tells us that "God will set up a kingdom that shall never be destroyed or delivered up to another people; rather it shall break in pieces all these kingdoms and put an end to them, and it shall last forever."

"Do not live in fear, little flock. It has pleased your Father to give you the kingdom" (Luke 12:32). Our Lord is here referring to the kingdom of truth, beauty and goodness the Church is, which shall last as long as time. She will never cease to be. Those who belong to her have no need for earthly glory, since by being Catholics they are made members of the household of the King, and so they have no need for any other kind of renown to make them happy. Their glory consists in the fact that they are Catholics, and that's glory enough for any man.

"Why do the nations rage and the peoples utter folly? The kings of the earth rise up and the princes conspire together against the Lord and against his anointed" (Ps. 2:1-2).

It is the Catholic Church the Psalmist has in mind, and it is in reference to the divine decrees which she promulgates that men have in all ages said:

"Let us break their fetters and cast their bonds from us" (Ps. 2:3).

Every single phase of the life of the Church is depicted in the Psalms, and it's of her they so sublimely sing. The Psalter has been named the Church's prayer book, and if we would know what the Church is like we have to read the Book of Psalms.

In the Book of Psalms, God gave us a method of prayer which has been especially devised by Him for the purpose of praising and glorifying the Church of Christ. All her good fortunes as well as misfortunes are there described, and in it we are assured by God Himself that it is her destiny to endure forever:

"Why do the nations rage and the peoples utter folly?"

It is in vain that anyone fights against the Church, for he is destined to be outlasted by her, and that nation never was, that kingdom and empire has never existed at whose demise and extinction she will fail to preside. What is any country existing today compared to the Catholic Church, and where will it be a thousand years from now? We should glory in the fact we are citizens of heaven—it is to the new Jerusalem that's above that we should take pride to belong.

The Church is Sion; she is Jerusalem and the City of God which all the saints have spoken of, and which St. John beheld descending from heaven. We are the inhabitants of that Jerusalem, the citizens of that City, and it is in this realization all our happiness lies. We rejoice to think that we are the members of a Church founded by Christ, who was the "beginning" in whom all things were created by God. "In the beginning God created the heavens and the earth." We now know that Christ is that "beginning" and without Him was made nothing that was made.

We seek in vain for an explanation of the universe without the Church, for it is in her alone it can ever be had. Like her Divine Founder, she is the "key of David" that will unlock for us the mysteries of heaven and earth and enable us to penetrate into the secret designs of God as regards the meaning and significance of everything that can come up in this life. She alone has the answer to every question a human being can ask in reference to the meaning and significance of life.

The Church was founded by God to minister to the spiritual, intellectual and moral needs of the human race, and no one is able to separate himself from her and remain indifferent to the doctrines she has been commissioned to teach. The Church is a Mother who is solicitous about the well-being of her children in a spiritual way. There is a great deal of mental and moral poison in the world today, and it is the function of the Church to point this out. It is not her function to prevent us from being physically harmed, but to protect us from the dangers the soul is able to incur. "Do not fear," she says to us, "those who deprive the body of life but cannot destroy the soul" (Matt. 10:28).

When we reflect on what a wonderful institution the Church is, we realize at once that she could have been brought into being only by God. "Set me as a seal on your heart," we hear her say to her divine Bridegroom, "as a seal on your arm; for stern as death is love, relentless as the nether world is devotion; its flames are a blazing fire." These words are mystically ascribed to the Catholic Church, for the love that's in her never dies, endowed as it is with the imprint of that which is divine. The Church has been called the mystical city of God, the Mystical Body of Christ, and she is the Sion mentioned so frequently in the Old Testament writings. It is she the Psalmist had in view when he said:

"If I forget you, O Jerusalem, may my right hand be forgotten! May my tongue cleave to my palate if I remember you not, If I place not Jerusalem ahead of my joy" (Psalm 136).

Von Galen, the great German Cardinal, once said, "We Von Galens are not particularly learned nor good-looking, but we have Catholicism in our bones." This is the kind of language we should love to hear spoken in reference to the Church, for it's only in this way our true appreciation of all she does for us can be expressed. All the saints loved the Church; they were all her devoted children and that's why they were always so happy and so cheerful. Cheerfulness or joy in the Lord is one of the outstanding characteristics of those who truly love God. Where this is missing there can be no true sanctity.

"Rejoice in the Lord," St. Paul tells us (Philip. 4:4), but we can only do this by being fervent Catholics and by loving the Church as all the saints have done. We can never take the Church for granted, and when we do so, our faith begins to die. "After all, I am a daughter of the Church." It was with these words the great St. Teresa of Avila used to console herself every time she was tempted to grow discouraged. There is nothing like the realization that we are Catholics to strengthen and buoy up the soul in all the trials that can come up in this life, for it is the reflection on this truth that does all this for us.

We are told in the book of Exodus that "Moses stretched out his hand toward the sky, and there was dense darkness throughout the land of Egypt. . . . Men could not see one another. . . . But all the Israelites had light where they dwelt" (Ex. 10:22).

In reading this passage and meditating upon it, it has always occurred to me that "Egypt" is a type of intellectual and moral darkness they are in who are outside the Church and that the "Israelites" are they who have the grace to belong to her. How many there are outside the Church who are perplexed as to why they had been born, why they live and why they die! They are in complete ignorance of the plan God has in creating the universe and of His placing us in it. They don't know why they were born and what will happen to them after they depart from this life, for the Church alone can give them a true and reasonable answer to this question. No other institution—no other religion is able to enlighten them on this point with the completeness and satisfaction she is able to give. To her alone has been vouchsafed the knowledge as to the destiny of our lot on this earth; she alone can tell us what will happen to us after we depart from it. She alone has received the full revelation on this matter from Almighty God. Christ died and rose again for this very purpose of enlightening us as to what will take place after we die.

A Catholic knows what will happen to him after he dies and he is assured of this by God Himself. Through his faith in the Church he receives the grace to know that there is a heaven, and he can know this in no other way, for the truths she teaches transcend the power of our reasoning faculties. We can arrive at a knowledge of them through her alone.

We have to reflect on this every time we think of the fact that we are Catholics, for in so doing, we will appreciate the gift of being able to belong to the only true Church.

WHAT IS HEAVEN LIKE?

To know what heaven is like, we have to pray for the grace to have some of its quality in ourselves. There is no other way that its joys may be experienced while we are still on earth. After this life is over, we will no longer stand in need of praying to God that He should be good enough to let some of its bliss flow into our soul, for we will then become so completely blended with it that we and it will become one and the same thing.

What is heaven but a state of bliss for which no other word can be found? What is heaven but a state of being to which the laws of geography do not apply? Heaven is not something to be understood by our feeble intellect, because the nature of it transcends anything we are able to conceive. Heaven is an experience of the soul to be had by grace alone. The philosophers are ignorant of the beauties that are there and the wondrous joys of which it is made up. The Jews of old referred to heaven as a "land flowing with milk and honey."

Heaven is something which may be found residing in the souls of the saints, just as the opposite may be detected in those who harbor a hatred for what is divine. "Myself am hell," the poet makes Satan say. What Milton made Satan say as regards the infernal regions, God causes the saints to exclaim, "Myself am heaven." St. Bernard assures us that "the soul of every just person may be truly called a heaven" (Commentary on the Song of Songs).

By means of grace we can even now experience in ourselves the joys we shall have after this life is over. St Teresa likens the world that the soul is, to a castle with many mansions. These mansions consist of the different degrees of love for and union with God. Let us ask God for the grace to be able to enter into this castle, and we will soon discover what the joys of heaven are like.

Heaven is close by. It is within ourselves, and so we have but to penetrate into the depths of our souls to find it there. It is because we are strangers to the inner riches of our own being that we find it so difficult to perceive what heaven is like. In the soul of every just person God has placed a Garden of Eden of inner riches, the fullness of which we shall never completely enjoy save when we leave this world. Still, there is a great deal of these riches which we may, if we so wish, enjoy in our present mortal state, for there would not have otherwise been said: "The reign of God is already in your midst" (Luke 18:21). We have but to seek for this heaven in the soul of every just person to find it mystically present there.

To know what heaven is like, we ourselves must become a kind of heaven, for like is known by like. "To know the Good God, we ourselves must become good," Saint Ambrose says. By becoming united with God we will be given the grace to experience the joys of heaven even while we are still in this life, and experiencing these joys we will get to know what heaven is like.

We can at present think of heaven only in terms of flesh, that one assumed by the Son of God, every other conception and experience thereof being too difficult to grasp. The Flesh of Christ is a true paradise filled with all manner of mystical delights. After the resurrection, the body we now have will in its glorified state share in the quality of that of our divine Lord.

We would like to know by personal experience what heaven is like, but the best way this can be done is to contemplate all our Lord is, both body and soul. Christ is heaven and the way thereto—He it is who will constitute its unending bliss. Christ came into this world to give us a true idea of what the joys of heaven are like, since by loving Him we get a taste of these joys. It's hard to talk of heaven while we are still on earth, and yet glimpses of its bliss continue to find their way into our weariness-laden lives.

WHAT IS MAN WITHOUT GOD?

We have to have a passion for Christ, otherwise our religious life won't do us any good. It's not enough to believe in God; we have to have a passion for the divine and make it the dominant force in our lives, since it's passion which governs the lives of men. Reason plays a minor role in them.

We all know what passion is, and that it has to be centered on someone or something. Men differ not in the reasons they have, but according to the particular passions they exercise toward everything with which they are brought into intimate relationship. The musician has a passion for his music, the painter for color and form, the writer for the beauty of words, and so on. But we Christians can only fully realize ourselves when we permit ourselves to be carried away by the passion for Him Whom we love and believe in so much. We cannot be Christians halfway and by our reasoning alone—to be true followers of Christ we have to be swept off our feet by the mere thought of all that He is. The saints were passionate cravers of the divine, that's why they had so much influence over others. Communists are passionately devoted to the doctrines they promulgate, and that is why they propagate them with such alarming success.

Passion is the key to the life of any successful person—he can be accounted for in no other way. What makes us pleasing to God is not so much the way we think of Him but the deep way we feel in our souls the beauty of His being. Moses was a passionate lover of the divine; that is why he accomplished so much in his dealings with his people. They followed him because of the burning ardor they perceived in his soul. It is ardor, passion, craving for the divine that distinguishes the saint from ordinary Christians. The enemies of the Church would be rendered helpless if all its members became passionate cravers of the divine and yearned for it.

It's all right for a silly girl to fall in love with a Hollywood actor, but one is looked upon with disdain if he yields himself up completely to Christ and loves Him in an intense passionate way. We must despise the world when it tells us it's all right to be passionately fond of what it has to offer, transitory and perishable goods, but that it's not all right to love with the same amount of passion, with the same degree of feeling, that which is everlasting.

In what passionate terms the prophets spoke, and how overwhelmed they were by things divine! "Hear, O heavens, and listen, O earth; for the Lord speaks. . . . An ox knows its owner, and an ass his master's manger; but Israel does not know. My people have not understood." (Is. 1:2-3). The prophet complains that there is little faith in the world and that the ardor for Christ has grown cold. "Israel does not know." he says, and by these words he means to imply that there is a deficiency in the living experience of things divine, and that things supernatural are not vivid and graphic enough.

We need more ardor and greater intensity as far as the things of faith are concerned, because in order that they may be perfectly appreciated they have to be passionately loved, as passionately at least as we love other things. Its easy to love what we see with the eyes of the body, but to love passionately what the mind alone is able to perceive, that is not so easy, and so great effort is required for it to be accomplished. It's easy to love a human being, but not so easy to love Him who is both God and Man. It's easy to be carried away by passing events, but to crave for things eternal is something limited to a few enlightened souls—they alone exert their passion for Christ.

We need prophets in the world and seers with mystic insight into the nature of things, so as by means of their visions to be carried away and swept off their feet by what is by the mercy of God made manifest to them. Like Saint Paul, we have to be "caught up into paradise." We need great men and great women whose hearts and minds are set aflame with passionate craving for things divine—this alone will be able to regenerate the world and bring it to the feet of Christ. "Turn, turn, O Shulamite" (Song of Songs, 7:1). Go back to Christ, these words say, from whom you have strayed. The soul is converted to God by spiritual hunger, by its passionate craving for things divine.

The world is very busy with itself, and so it has no time for Him by whom it has been made. Stand aside, it says to God, for I am too taken up with my own well-being. The Creator of the universe is relegated to a minor role in the lives of men, and it's this realization which renders the lives of the saints so bitter.

Men find it hard to believe Christ is God. It is incredible to them that the Incarnation should have occurred. This is because they cannot let themselves be carried away by the wonder of that Mystery, and to be overawed and overwhelmed by it. We will never really enjoy being Catholics until the sense of wonder grows strong enough to overwhelm the mind, so that it not only thinks and reflects, but feels passionately in reference to all that has to be believed.

There is a defeatism in the world today because men lack courage to love God with their whole heart. There is a halfheartedness as regards the things of faith. We have to have daring to express openly our belief in Christ Jesus. This is the only way in which we can be truly happy and at peace in this life.

"I looked at the earth, and it was waste and void; at the heavens, and their light had gone out" (Jerem. 4:28). In these words the prophet points out that without Christ nothing has any meaning, for it's only belief in the divine which gives anything the reality and value it deserves. What is man without God? What is all he does without belief in His Only Begotten Son? What's the use of having lived if we do not live for the things over which death has no jurisdiction?

BEAUTY IS GOD'S REFLECTION

All beautiful things in this world are of service to man only insofar as they lead him to the beauty of Christ. God made the world and all things in it to be a means to Himself, for this and no other reason. With this in view, when we look at a beautiful object, we should do so with the realization that the beauty in it is meant to raise the heart and mind to God.

In the mind of the mystics, all things in this world are a kind of ladder to the Creator of them. Beautiful things fascinate the heart, and so, as we go on living, we must learn how to extract the essence of beauty in things beautiful. We must learn to love beauty itself and as it exists apart from these things—in Christ Jesus. However, it requires grace to be able to love the beauty inherent in things beautiful, and so apart from grace this cannot be done.

As we progress on the road to life eternal, we must look at all things as they exist in God and love them in Himself. As we go on living it becomes more and more important to love all things on this earth in the same way as they do who are already in heaven, that is to say, in our divine Lord.

Christ is the principle of beauty in all things beautiful, and so, loving Him, we love these things aright, as they are in truth. There is a passage in the Scriptures which reads, "Vanity of vanities, says Qoheleth, vanity of vanities! All things are vanity" (Ecclesiastes 1:1). In Hebrew, this word "vanity" implies the idea of illusion and deceptiveness, the deceptiveness all created things have in themselves. And so, loving them amiss, we love a lie.

Only Christ is real to a thinking and believing human being. All things outside of Him posses only an apparent reality. We are real in Christ Jesus, and all beautiful things are truly beautiful in Him alone. The saints became what they were because they loved all things in Him by whom they were brought into being.

Beauty ensnares the heart of man, we are told in the Scriptures. However, beauty may also be used to ensnare the heart with the beauty of Christ. By means of the beauty we see, we can become enraptured with God's own beauty. Christ is the principle of beauty in things beautiful. And so, to live aright, we should ask for the grace to love Him in these things.

Beauty is God's gift to the human race, and so we should make use of it to raise our hearts and minds to Him. There was a saint who saw the image of Christ in the beautiful things around him, such as the great masterpieces of painting and sculpture (Blessed Contardo Ferrini). In our effort to know Christ in a deeply intimate way, we should do the same thing.

Every time we see something to enrapture the heart, we must make use thereof as a means of becoming united with God and love Him in what we behold. Everything carries in itself a message from on high. By realizing this truth we can all become what the great saints have been—God being rich enough to make saints of us all. We can all be saints by allowing ourselves to be transfigured in Christ. By everything we see, we can raise up our hearts and minds to Him, thus identifying ourselves with all He Himself is. By loving Christ, we become what we love.

It is important that we should learn how to love all things in a deeply Christian manner—in our divine Lord. Thus loved, the things we love become a source of union for us with His own Sacred Person. There are so many things in the world to raise up our hearts and minds to God that it is inexcusable for us not to get to know God in a deeply intimate way. There are so many ways in which, by the beauty that's in them, we can be brought to the feet of Jesus.

St. Augustine tells us that God gave us eyes to see the things He has made and a mind with which to perceive the Maker of them. We cannot be excused from not loving the principle of beauty in all things beautiful. We cannot claim exemption from the obligation of adoring Christ by means of the beautiful things He has brought into being. We cannot be

excused from not loving God, seeing He has so lavishly
instilled His own beauty in everything around us.

By means of the things seen with the eyes of the body we
are led to the apprehension of a type of loveliness which can
only be perceived by the mind. Through what we see, we
learn to love what is not disclosed to the eyes of the body.
We can live in eternity right now by loving all things in Him
in Whom they subsist as in their source and principle.

God is easy to love, since He has so munificently left traces
of Himself in all existing things. Why don't more people love
God? we are often tempted to ask. It's so easy to do so, seeing
they have the Lord and Creator right in themselves. When
we meet God in the next life we will clearly see how He has
been in ourselves from the first instant of our existence.

Oh, how wearisome it gets merely to talk about God or
even just to believe in Him. What the soul craves in its deep
inner self is to be what God is. We cannot be satisfied until
we become by means of grace that which God Himself is. We
yearn for death, though in a holy way, thus to become what
God Himself is. Death alone can make possible the identifi-
cation between God and ourselves. It's only by means of our
bodily demise we will be able to say, "My lover belongs to me
and I to him" (Song of Songs 2:16).

EARTHLY LOVE REFLECTS GODLY LOVE

To know God in the right way we have to love a great deal. It's only those who have affectionate natures that are capable of experiencing all the delight divine things have. God is not loved because few know the true nature of His being. Few know Him to be pure beauty, pure truth and pure love. Many know God, but they do so in a purely theoretical manner, in a manner in which it is insufficient for them to make Him the mainstay of their lives. Many believe in God, but they do not know Him by personal experience—it's the personal experience of the divine that can fill up that void in our makeup which cannot be understood by our mind. Many know God through the instructions they receive of Him either by word of mouth or the books they read, but this kind of knowledge lacks that deep personal note they have who dispose their souls for all the graces it is God's will they should receive.

Many love God and have a certain limited understanding of His being, but it's not enough to set their souls afire and be consumed thereby. Such people fail to impress others as to who and what God is, namely, eternal delight and everlasting wonderfulness.

Many love God, but it's love of a very mediocre kind, and so neither they nor those around them find themselves overimpressed. It's the love that burns and totally consumes us that really counts, and which alone has the power in it to satisfy all the cravings of our nature for what no other thing God has made is able to give us.

God is not known to the extent He should be and that's why men are so unhappy in this life. They fail to find a motive for living, and so their life has no meaning.

We can all love something that's genuinely beautiful, such as a beautiful painting, a beautiful statue, a beautiful landscape, a beautiful face and a beautiful thought. The love of all these can and should lead to the love of Him Who is the ALL-Beautiful One Christ is, and whom the Psalmist designates as being "fairer . . . than the sons of men" (Ps 45:3).

The love we have for things beautiful can be converted into a passionate love for Christ, from whom all this beauty proceeds as from its source. "From the greatness and the beauty of created things their original author, by analogy is seen" (Wisdom 13:5). We can all love something that touches the heart with the grace and charm which is in that thing, and so no excuse can be made for the lack in ourselves of a passionate love for what is transcendent and divine.

The saints loved the beauty in things beautiful; that's why they became such ardent lovers of the divine—they developed in themselves a capacity to detect the divine in all things. "In a certain sense," said one of them, "I find His name printed on every page I read, find Him in every achievement of the arts, in every achievement of genius, in every revelation of divine ideas that reaches me through the human spirit. From every masterpiece His fragrance comes out to me. Many times in the museums of Monaco, Dresden, Berlin, Vienna, Rome, Florence, I found myself caught by His Beauty when I stood before some pictures or sculpture: in my admiration of what man has done I almost wept to think of the immeasurably greater achievements that God must be able to do" (Blessed Contardo Ferrini). Every believer in Christ should have a spot in his heart for the beauty of Christ that exists in all things beautiful, so that he may by their means be brought closer to Him.

There are not enough of us who have mastered the art of being able to love the beauty of God in all things beautiful—that is why the love for Him is so utterly ineffectual. We have to love Christ with intense passion, for we will otherwise be led astray by the beauty we find in things beautiful. "Tell me, you whom my heart loves, where you pasture your flock, where you give them rest at midday, lest I be found wandering after the flocks of your companions" (Song of Songs 1:7). Unless we are carried away by the love for things eternal, we will find ourselves completely absorbed by what is of a nature to pass away with time.

God loves us passionately, and so why should we not love Him in the same way? God loves us unto the death of the Cross, and are we to pick and choose as to how much we should bear out of love for Him? Shall we stand by and be outdone in this by those who spend themselves on the things that have to have an end with time? Shall we let others love things that are made more than we do what will never have an end? Shall we stand by and see creatures loved more ardently than we do the Creator of these creatures?

How can we say it's hard to love God when there are so many good and beautiful things by which this can be done? What is God but the goodness and beauty in these things?

By loving the beauty in things beautiful we rise to a knowledge of Him by whom these have been brought into being. We don't have to become philosophers to love God, but just observers—everything at which we can look has something divine in its makeup, and the same is able to lead us to Him as by so many steps.

We journey to Him by the sight of all the good and beautiful things existing all around us, including our own being. It's this manner of knowing God that's important, since it leads to a direct form of communication with what is divine. It leads to a love of God that is passionate and ardent—we have to be overwhelmed by Christ, for we will otherwise never get to know Him in the right way, the way all the saints have done.

God has placed in everything an indication of Himself—a trace as it were of His own being. If we were wise, we would seek Him out. Everything that exists can tell us something about Him by whom it has been brought into being. The saints heard the voice of God speak to them out of everything that has been made; that is why they became so intimately acquainted with what is divine. In everything that has been made something can be detected which will always surpass the power of the mind to comprehend—something inexplicable and mysterious will always be present in all created things, and this will always be a cause for wonderment and admiration. All things have something mysterious in their makeup, and so our reflection upon them will lead us to God.

LOVING JESUS IN HIS FLESH

All the saints loved Jesus. That's why they became what they were. The saints became that which they loved. Love made them one with the Object of their love. Do we wish to become what God Himself is? Let us love Him the way the saints loved Him. The saints loved Jesus to excess. If we wish to become what the saints were we must imitate them in this respect—that of loving the Flesh of Christ without any limits.

There is something mystical about the flesh of a human being. This is due to the fact that the God-Man assumed this flesh unto Himself, thus rendering it sacred. Every human being bears in himself something of the nature of the Godhead. Every human being carries in his makeup the image of Christ. Every human being is worthy of reverence because of the fact of Christ's dying for him. Every human being has that in his interior makeup worthy of veneration. In dying for him, God has Himself shown respect for the inner makeup of a human being.

He does so by the fact that in the Person of His Son He suffered for him. We cannot honor enough that in ourselves by which we resemble God. We cannot revere ourselves enough from this point of view. From the point of view of Christ, every human being that lives is worthy of our utmost esteem, reverence and respect.

By taking our flesh, Christ shares Himself with us—He became what we ourselves are. The Incarnation has bridged the barrier between time and eternity. We don't have to die to become immortalized. We already are so in Christ Jesus. Living in Jesus, we already exist as if we were no longer in this life.

Our faith in Him and our love for Him have enabled us to transcend all earthly limitations. What is heaven like? The answer to this question consists in one single word: Jesus.

Jesus is heaven. And so loving Him, we are already there. We are already there in that part of ourselves immune to the laws of time and change.

By loving Jesus we become changeless in Jesus. Jesus has now become our life, and so loving Him, we love what shall for all eternity remain lovable. To be happy in this life, we have to love what shall never have an end. Christ is the Endless One; in loving Him, we take on the quality of His own endlessness.

Christ is beauty made Flesh. Loving that beauty of His, we become beautiful with His own beauty. We become beautiful with the Beauty of the God-Man. In the Person of His Son, God has enshrined Himself in our own human nature. In it, God has made Himself visible in the flesh. He did this by becoming what we ourselves are. Do we wish to become beautiful with Christ's own beauty? If we do, let us love this Beauty of His in a sort of infinite way and to the exclusion of every other thing.

By loving Christ, we love that in ourselves which shall last forever. By loving Christ we become what we love. Let us adore the sacred Flesh of the Son of God and reverence it in ourselves. There is a Christlike quality in every human being, and it's this quality in each we must revere and esteem.

Man is not worth loving for what he is in himself alone, that is, without and apart from Him by whom he has been redeemed. Take away Christ, and what becomes of a human being? Christ makes us real to ourselves. Without Him, we are but fleeting images. Without Him, we are mere phantoms. "Vanity of vanities! All things are vanity" (Ecclesiastes 1:2). Without Christ, our existence becomes illusory and vain.

Every part of the Body of Christ was divine. It is in this realization that both our salvation and sanctification lies. We are sanctified by partaking of the Flesh of Christ, as well as in all the numberless ways by which we are brought into intimate relationship with Him. We cannot talk adequately of the beauty of Christ's Sacred Flesh. Anything we can say in reference to it, does not approximate what the beauty of that Flesh is in its glorified Form.

St. Paul tells us that "In Christ the fullness of deity resides in bodily form" (Col. 2:9). This is sufficient to make us realize how infinitely transcendent the Person of our Lord is and how sweetly and how awesomely He should be contemplated by us. We resemble the God-Man, and this because of the fact of His assuming our own human nature. How wonderfully sweet it is to think of Christ and to contemplate the infinite beauty of His Being!

When we contemplate Christ, we at the same time contemplate our own existence. When we contemplate Christ, we contemplate infinite beauty made Flesh. God is sweet to contemplate in the Person of His Son Jesus. When we have the grace to pronounce His Sacred Name, we get an idea of what the joys of the next life are like. We taste these joys when we think of Christ in a loving way and when we are properly disposed to the Christian religion. We become saints by being incorporated into the God of love.

We cannot think deeply enough of Him who became Man for our sake. We cannot love Jesus enough. We cannot have a sufficient amount of love for the Sacred Flesh of the God-Man. To love Christ in the right way, we have to undergo the transfiguration of Mount Tabor and be raised up to the regions above. As the result of the Incarnation, the flesh we now bear about us will become completely trans-figured in Christ Jesus.

In our deep inner selves we can become what God Himself is, and enjoy what cannot be described. We cannot have enough love for the Flesh of Jesus. There is something in ourselves that resembles Him by whom we have been created. The saints longed for death so that they could in that way become commingled with the Flesh of Christ. We cannot in this life become all that Christ Himself is. It's for this reason we look forward to going home to heaven.

We long to be where Jesus is in His glorified state. We want to be glorified with Him, and this we cannot have in the present life. We are dissatisfied with faith alone. We want to be there toward which this faith of ours points. It points in the direction of the celestial regions. We won't be satisfied until we become by grace, or glory rather, all that Jesus Himself is. This is what the Psalmist had in view when he said, "I shall be satisfied when thy glory shall appear" (Ps. 17:15, Septuagint translation).

It is no small ambition a Christian has. He wants to be what the Founder of that religion Himself was. Does it not say in the Scriptures, "I have said, You are gods" (John 10:34). We become what God Himself is when we get the grace to live the Sacred Humanity of our divine Lord, and to revel in the beauty of His Being. How beautiful Christ is! The Psalmist tells us that there is no beauty like the one possessed by the Son of God (Ps. 45:3).

We cannot love Jesus enough. We cannot sufficiently adore His Sacred Flesh. We want to die so that we may in that way be able to adore the Sacred Flesh of Christ in the manner that It merits to be adored. Until the end of time men will go on realizing that they are nothing apart from Christ. Without Christ this whole universe is nothing but some vast chimera.

Christ endows all things with the being they have. We must realize this as we think of Christ. For all eternity we shall reap the reward of our faith in Christ and love for Him all the time we were in this life. With this in view, let us permit ourselves to be made beautiful with the beauty of the God-Man. Let us love Jesus as they do who are already in heaven. Thus loved, we will be given the grace to even now become what we will one day be in Himself. We can even now become what Jesus is, so as to be commingled with Him in a wonderful way.

By loving the Sacred Flesh of our divine Lord, we become one with that Flesh. Becoming one with the Flesh of Christ, what is there in this life we would want to have which cannot be ours? Let us love Jesus in a way too marvelous to be expressed in words. Let us love the Flesh of Christ in ourselves.

THE TRUE LIFE

"Have no love for the world,
nor the things that the world affords.
If anyone loves the world,
The Father's love has no place in him."

(I John 2:15)

Rarely do we hear these words spoken today anywhere. We don't hear them in our churches. That's why so many are deceived in their pursuit of happiness and seek it where it was not meant by God to be had. The world is a natural enemy of all the Spirit stands for, all it longs for, of all its aspirations, and so anyone who fill up his heart and mind with what the world has to offer has no room in himself for the things of Christ.

The world and God cannot be reconciled save by means of the reconciliation Christ is. But what is that reconciliation? It consists in the renunciation of all that is not of a nature to last forever, all temporal things, and in the making use of them, but not in the setting of our hearts upon them. God breaks the hearts of those who love Him; He despoils them of all their hopes and causes them to be cast aside by the world.

All the saints were failures as far as the things of this life are concerned—they gloried in their misfortunes and considered them the exact opposite of what the world holds them to be. The saints were always reminded that in the words of the poet Rilke, they had "no home in time." It was to the grave the saints loved to go, since there they found answers to all their questions, and comfort for all their sorrows.

The world and its vanities have rooted themselves in the hearts of men and women, so that only the grace of Christ is able to remove them—it does this by means of suffering. Suffering clears away the haze from the eyes of the soul, and it's only when this haze is removed that we can see things in their proper perspective. Christ and the world are totally different. The world misleads, and He does not. The world holds up a different set of values from those He came to bring. The world says education will save our souls, but what is all the learning without the saving grace of our divine Lord? The world says that life is good and that its pleasures are to be enjoyed to the full. However, those of us who exercise our reason instead of our emotions know differently.

We know that mere pleasure is false and that it cannot give what we crave so much, deep interior peace and joy. It takes time, but sooner or later we all learn the lesson that the world is deceitful and that all its hopes end up in the grave. What are all pleasures which last but for a brief second? Are they worthy of an intelligent human being, made as he is in the image of God, that is to say, capable of everlasting happiness in heaven?

From early childhood, the world exercises a false charm over us. We are miseducated and led to believe we can find salvation in this life alone, and that heaven can be had while still on earth. Fame stalks the soul, and everyone we meet is engaged in the pursuit of what will bring him esteem in the eyes of others who are equally misled.

We are taught to look down on the poor and admire those who possess material riches—this produces a kind of poison in the soul, from the effects of which few recover. Only the saints are not taken in by this kind of falsehood; they alone are aware of the true values of life. All people want to be admired and praised; they strive for what will bring them renown. Truth is shunned, and so men and women pursue a different set of values from those to be found in the Old and New Testament writings.

What is the world we are asked not to love? It is certainly not the one God has made. It is not the world of nature, the earth, with all the things on it. It is not the heavens with all its myriads of stars and planets. It is not something physical that we are told not to love. The world we are told not to love is the one created by the thoughts of men and women, their wrong desires and pursuits. We are told not to set our hearts upon anything human beings have made and which is of a nature to pass away with time.

We make a fuss about a lot of things which have no relevance for eternity, and it's these we are told not to love, when we are told not to love the world, the world made by men and women, their interests, concerns and values which bear no significance apart from time.

Men and women love themselves, and loving themselves, they have no room in their hearts for the love of Christ. We die when we set our hearts on what must end up in the grave, our mortal part, that part of ourselves not made in the image of God, but in the likeness of the lower creatures. We die when we love power and material riches, which the world holds in such high esteem. Christ is the life the saints value, and this life does not end up at the foot of the grave.

WHY THE SAINTS WANTED TO DIE

How can we express in words the love that's in us for Jesus Christ? We cannot. And so we have to die to be able to do so. The saints wanted to die so that they could in that way give utterance to the love that's in them for the God-Man. If we were as holy as they, we would want to do the same thing. If we wish to know the yearning in the hearts of the saints for our divine Love, we have to turn to the writings of the saints, since they alone were given the grace to be able to express in words what that yearning was.

The saints had personal experience with Christ, and it was for this reason they all longed to die. How could they go on living with the beauty of that vision of Him in their hearts? They could not. It was only by the aid of God's special grace that they were enabled to bear their earthly state. It was only their love for Christ that gave them the impetus to be able to endure their existence in time.

How the writings of the saints refresh us, with the sweet, sublime and beautiful way they all speak of Christ! It's enough to make us weary of living when we read their words—we want to be with Him of whom they speak so beautifully. One saint is worth more than a thousand ordinary Christians, and this because of the tremendous love the saints have in their hearts for Him who is love in nature and essence.

The saints alone count as far as God is concerned, and it's only in proportion as we become like them that we take on worth in His eyes. We should read all the saints have to say in reference to our divine Lord, for it's they alone who really know Him. It's they alone who really love Him, and who are given the grace to penetrate the secrets of His heart.

If we are saints, we succeed as far as our love for Christ is concerned. We should read the words of love the saints used in reference to our divine Lord. If we will do so, we will be ashamed of the poverty of our own regard for Him.

We must go to the saints for everything in the way of knowledge, wisdom and love, since they alone are the true possessors thereof. No one knows Christ the way the saints have known Him. No one is able to love Him with the same degree of ardor and intensity. Compared with that love, ours is only so much sham and counterfeit. In a word, the saint is everything as far as Christ is concerned. We who are not saints are only tolerated by Him on account of the saints. By the intensity of their love, they compensate Christ for the love He does not get from us.

I am reading the writings of Saint Gertrude the Great, and as I do so, I am amazed to find how sweet and beautiful they are. After reading all she has to say in reference to our divine Lord, one is tempted never to look at anything else that has been written about Him, so transcendentally superior is all she has to say compared with all the others. How dear to the Heart of Christ this saint was! How refreshing and strengthening to the soul her words are, and how they fill it with the same desire she herself had for her divine Bridegroom!

We should not be able to rest in this life until we ask God to become as great a saint as anyone who ever lived. Unless we become saints, it is in vain we are Christians. We are Christians so that we may in that way possess all the saints possessed all the time they had been in this life, and which same was their knowledge and love of Jesus Christ.

We should become saints to honor Christ and to glorify His Father who is in heaven. We don't become saints for our own glory but for the glory of Him by and through whom we are all we are. By becoming saints, we render to Christ the kind of love we could give Him in no other way. We cannot render this glory to Him by remaining ordinary Christians with ordinary love in our hearts for the things of the Spirit.

LOVING THE SCRIPTURES

"In the beginning . . . God created the heavens and the earth" (Genesis 1:1). What falsehood and errors these words will forever destroy! We do not have to become perplexed as we contemplate the physical universe, wondering how it came to be and by whom. "In the beginning, etc." God Himself constitutes that "beginning" in the person of His divine Son, who says to us in the Gospel that He is the "beginning" (John 8:25).

How these sublime and simple words which open up the Book of Genesis have fascinated the minds and hearts of all the saints! How they thanked God who has Himself inspired them to be written down. What insane falsehoods have been advanced as to how the world came to be, and with what power and beauty these words eradicate such intellectual and philosophical deceits!

"In the beginning . . . God created the heavens and the earth." How majestically musical is the sound of these words in the original Hebrew! That ancient Hebrew tongue characterized by the rabbis of old as the "sacred language." We linger over the sound of these words as we do over the strains of music by the great masters such as Bach and Beethoven. Nothing written equals the majesty and sublimity of the Holy Scriptures, and so we should read them kneeling in prayer. Have not all the saints read the word of God in this manner? Should we ourselves not entertain the same love and regard for what will for all time remain the greatest book that has ever been written?

We cannot love the Scriptures enough, all the saints and doctors of the Church have told us, since in them we have the Lord Himself for our Master and Guide. We cannot be grateful enough to God to have inspired them to be written for our consolation. How many human problems the Scriptures solve! What an infinite amount of perplexing questions are answered by them regarding the meaning of this life! The Scriptures tell us why we came into this world and why we will one day have to make our departure from it.

"It is He that made us, and not we ourselves," we are told in the old vulgate translation of Psalm 100:3. We do not have to perplex ourselves as to how we came to be and by Whom and through Whom and in Whom. We came to be through Him who always is. By loving God we become eternalized with Him. We know by faith that just as it is He who made the world we see with the eyes of the body, so He is the One who created the world which exists in our hearts and minds—which is infinitely more beautiful than the physical universe.

There is a world within, the saints tell us, and it is this interior being in ourselves on which we must center the love of our hearts and minds, and which we must ask God for the grace to be able to contemplate. It's easy to admire outward grandeur and outward beauty. It's not so easy to love and esteem what cannot be disclosed to our physical sight.

There is a world within and one without and they have both been brought into being by the Lord of Creation. "O come, let us worship and bow down, let us kneel before the Lord our Maker . . . It is He that made us and not we ourselves." How divinely assuring these words are, and what balm from on high they bring with them! How many look for peace and happiness in this life without ever attaining them? Do they love the Scriptures? we ask in reference to all such. No one has ever failed to be protected by almighty God who has turned to Him for such protection.

"You who dwell in the shelter of the Most High, who abide in the shadow of the Almighty, say to the Lord, 'My refuge and my fortress' " (Psalm 91:1-2). We cannot have enough faith in God, these words say to us. We cannot have a sufficient amount of confidence and hope in His goodness and love, seeing, as we must, that this goodness and love is infinite in scope.

"Who has ever trusted in the Lord and been forsaken by him?" it says in the Scriptures. We cannot have enough faith that God will in His goodness and love see us through all the trials of this life, so that when it's over we shall be brought to the happy end heaven will be for the kind of existence in which we now find ourselves. We love the Scriptures and turn to them because such a hope is grounded in them. In their inspired words we find solutions to the problems that come up in this life. In them, we find answers to the question of who and what we are. We are there told what will happen to us when we die. We are there told that upon our departure from this life we shall be with God forever and ever.

WITHOUT CHRIST, ONLY DARKNESS

"Tell me, you whom my heart loves, where you pasture your flock, where you give them rest at midday" (Song of Songs 1:7).

Christ is the bright Luminary of man's spiritual and intellectual world, and without the grace which His blessed coming brought into the world, we live in darkness, that is to say, in ignorance of God the Father and Creator of all existing things.

In order to be happy we have to have the Light our Lord is and the grace which illuminates the sad and unhappy regions of our own being. With this in view, it's no wonder Christ calls Himself the light of the world, and "light," in Hebrew, has the added meaning of cheerfulness and joy. It signifies the idea of that happiness and well-being the soul experiences only by belief in Him.

The soul asks for "rest at midday." In so doing it requests the tranquil security which belief in the supernatural brings with it. How serene and calm are those who believe in Christ! How disturbed and agitated they are who, through their own fault, lack such a grace! The "wicked," the Prophet tells us, "are like the tossing sea which cannot be calmed, And its waters can be mud and filth. No peace for the wicked! says my God" (Isaiah 57:20).

Belief in Christ brings its reward of peace and rest for the soul, and they know it not to whom the Son of God is a stranger. The soul is always praying for light from God in order to know itself better each day. As long as we live, we cannot have too much of the light of Christ, and so we keep on asking for it all the time.

We cannot love God too much in this life, so the words of this song cannot be too frequently in our heart and mind. We long for the mystical rest which faith in Christ is for the soul, and we shall continue doing this to our dying day. It is one thing to love the creature, and quite another the Creator. The creature leads us to love Him by whom it has been made. In our inner being, we have to journey on until we are face to face with Him who is our ALL.

There is danger of finding rest in the things which God has made and not in Him. Creatures are enticing, and so they can be of harm by keeping us away from God. Due to the goodness and beauty in them, there is danger that instead of worshipping God we may stumble into the misfortune of falling down in adoration before the things which have been made.

The Jews of old fell into this sin when they made a golden calf, and the Greeks by carving their beautiful statues. Men and women are always falling down in adoration before things which have been made.

The words of the Song have been written to remind us of this fact. They tell us that we should long for Christ, and not for what has been brought into being on account of and through Him. They say that if the things of God are good and beautiful, then how much more so is He by whom they have been brought into being.

We should reflect on this truth so that by so doing we may avoid the mistake of "wandering after the flocks of our companions." By "companions" is meant all the good and beautiful things God has made. We must ask for the grace not to be sidetracked and distracted by the beauty we see with the eyes of the body, but to center our gaze on what is evident to the soul alone.

We beseech God for the grace not to look upon "what is seen but on what is unseen. What is seen is transitory; what is unseen lasts forever" (2 Corinthians 4:18). It is easy to love visible goods, and by so doing we lose the capacity to love those which are invisible.

It is so easy for the soul to want to settle down in this world and to look upon it as our home. It requires special grace not to be enticed by the beauty we see with the eyes of the body.

RUNNING AWAY FROM OURSELVES

Does this me every woman does
Not run away from Herself?

Everyone we meet seems to be engaged in the task of running away from himself—the things and places being as varied as those who do the running. In order to escape from themselves, some turn to travel, others to literature; others go to the arts, while others still turn to the performance of philanthropic deeds. Some turn to sinful pleasures.

It's all in vain. They are bound to meet themselves no matter where they go, or what object of diversion they seek for escape. Christ is the refuge of the soul, and only in Him *God* can we seek our escape. "You are my shelter," the Psalmist said a very long time ago. This holds true today as it did then (Ps. 32:7). We cannot escape the many miseries of our fallen nature unless we turn to Christ—He is the physician who alone can heal all our ills, whether of body or soul. Money cannot help us. We need the unpurchasable Good that Christ is to be truly happy and at peace in this life.

We build houses to live in and deck them out with splendor of every kind. But the occupants will be the same miserable people who moved into them. "Happy the man," the Psalmist says, "who follows not the counsel of the wicked nor walks in the way of sinners, nor sits in the company of the insolent" (Ps. 1:1). It is interesting to note that the Hebrew for "happy" or "blessed" is a synonym for "righteous," the implication being that we cannot be happy unless we live godly and upright lives. We cannot find happiness in exterior things, but only in what is interior and spiritual, these words hint to us.

The just man lives by faith, and it's Christ who justifies the just man, enabling him to have happiness and peace both here and forever afterward. We must not speak in the language of the world but in that of heaven and the happiness awaiting us there. We must not flee to the things of earth for happiness but to what is eternal and undying. We have been made for the immortal, but on the condition that we regard with disdain the fleeting pleasures of life. We have to run away from ourselves in order to be truly happy, but the refuge we must seek is Christ the Lord.

Christ is the true habitation of the heart and mind, so running away from one locality to another is not going to bring about any change in the state of our lives. No matter where we go, we will find our old selves again. The only reasonable thing to do then is to look for the kind of salvation our Lord came to bring. Christ eradicates us, and so we live in Him: "the life I live now is not my own; Christ is living in me" (Gal. 2-20).

Christ substitutes Himself for us and takes our place. He gives us His own new being in place of our own miserable one, so that His life becomes our life. We exchange ourselves with Him and, in so doing, get rid of all our miseries—He assimilates us into Himself. We can at present be only partially His, and our misery consists in the fact that we cannot now be completely Christ's—that there is a great deal in us which is not exclusively His.

Some 3,000 years ago, there lived a man who sought to find happiness in the possession of material riches. He was enormously wealthy, so he was able to give vent to his every desire. He did what so many foolishly do today. "I built myself houses and planted vineyards . . . I made gardens and parks . . . And I constructed for myself reservoirs to water a flourishing woodland. I acquired male and female slaves . . . I amassed for myself silver and gold . . . I became great, and I stored up more than all others before me in Jerusalem; my wisdom, too, stayed with me. Nothing that my eyes desired did I deny them, nor did I deprive myself of any joy . . . But when I turned to all the works my hands had wrought, and to the toil at which I had taken such pains, behold! all was vanity and a chase after wind" (Ecclesiastes 2:4-11).

We cannot find happiness in material things. No matter how beautiful the houses we build, they are powerless to give us what we really crave—dead matter has no power to satisfy the living soul. This is the sad tragedy of today, as well as of ages gone by. We are blinded to the real good Christ is. We see only the false and corruptible.

The devil seals the eyes of the soul, so that it may not see the infinite beauty of the Son of God. He tells us we should be content with chasing after the wind all created things are. He tells us to run away from ourselves, but not to flee to the refuge, the heaven of goodness and beauty Christ is. He bids us to escape, but not to God. The devil does not want us to be happy, that's why there are so many miserable people in the world—they go to him for advice. They read books he inspires men and women to write.

Satan is old hat, but he has a way of renewing himself by means of falsehoods and errors peculiar to each age in history. He is always engaged in the task of deceiving people, and this under the appearance of good.

THE DAY THAT FAITH ENDS

We won't take our faith with us into heaven, because we won't need it there—heaven consists in not having to have faith.

When we build an arch, we place props under it to keep the stones in place. But when the arch is finished, these are removed. The same thing applies to the house in heaven we build by means of faith. When at the point of death this house will be finished and we will enter into it, we won't need the prop our faith has been. Even during this life God sometimes takes away some of the props our faith has been. Even during this life, we sometimes see that which we believe, though we do so in a dark manner, confused and indistinct. Even during this life we see God, but the distinctness of His being is hidden from our view. In heaven we will see God not by faith but by sight. This is what the Psalmist means when he says, "And in your light we see light" (36:10).

During this life, God involves everything with Himself, so that we cannot see Him apart from that which has been made. After death a separation will be made between God and the creatures brought into being by Him. We now depend upon creatures for a knowledge of their Creator, but after this life is over, there will be no need for their mediation. We will then know God in God. It is this kind of knowledge of God the soul asks when she says to Christ, "Let him kiss me with the kisses of this mouth! More delightful is your love than wine" (Song of Songs 1:2). The request of the soul in this song is for Essentiality—an experience of the Divine not based upon faith but upon sight. The soul here prays for a mystical vision of the divine Good Jesus is.

This life is a pilgrimage, but it is a pilgrimage from faith to sight. We start out believing and end up seeing that which we believe. We are at present journeying to another world, and we do so by means of faith—belief is a road on which we travel to God.

Just as we cannot separate form from matter, so in this life we cannot know God apart from that which has been made by Him. We cannot separate ourselves from God in this life, for He constitutes the underlying essence of our being. Still, there is a need in the soul to know God as He exists in Himself and apart from anything which has been made—we call this mystical knowledge of the Divine Nature, and we long for it with our whole heart.

Death will satisfy this craving in us in a clear and perfect way—separated from the body to which it is now united, the soul will be able to see God more distinctly. The veil that faith is, will then be removed, and we shall know ourselves "even as we are known." As long as she remains in the body, the soul cannot be satisfied with the kind of knowledge faith alone gives and so she prays that this faith be supplemented by sight. The soul longs to see and not merely to believe. She longs for the Reality and not the shadow of that Reality.

She craves for the Substance and not its empty form. The soul wants God, but she longs for Him in Himself. She longs for the Divine devoid of any transient good. As long as she is in this life, the soul longs for God—everything that she sees reminds her of Him. The beauty of the creatures whets her appetite for the beauty of their Creator. In the words of the Song, she begs and entreats, "Tell me," she says to God, "you whom my heart loves, where you pasture your flocks, where you give them rest at midday . . . " (Song of Songs 1:7).

These are the words of the anguished soul, stricken by love for the uncreated beauty of God. The soul here longs for Christ—she says no one but He alone will ever be able to satisfy her, and fill up the need in herself for the kind of love which is infinitely lovable. The soul asks that the shadow faith be removed, so that it may give way to the substantial Good God is. The soul longs for truth, goodness and beauty as it is in itself, that is to say, sheer truth, sheer goodness and sheer beauty. The soul is willing to take leave of the body so that she may in that way see God as He exists in Himself.

Life is a struggle for the saints, because they have to live by faith and not by sight. The saints long for the kind of union with God that can only be had after this life is over—they pass their time in a state of mourning. "By the streams of Babylon we sat and wept when we remembered Sion. On the aspens of that land we hung up our harps," they say with the Psalmist (137:1-2). The saints look upon this world as a vale of tears, and so no amount of pleasures and satisfactions they may have is able to change their attitude. "How," they ask, "shall we sing a song of the Lord in a foreign land?" (Ps. 137:4). The saints want to go home, that is why they can never be at ease in this life.

The saints long for the joys of heaven, they know by instinct that nothing created will ever be able to satisfy them. The 137th Psalm was written to express the longing in the hearts of the saints for their home in heaven. "Woe is me," they say in the same psalm, "that I sojourn in Meshech" (120:5). In these words the saints complain that their life in this world is so long and drawn-out (Meshech, in Hebrew, signifying this prolongation of it). The saints long to be where it will no longer be necessary for them to exercise their faith—they wish to see that which they believe. The saints plead with God to take them out of this world—'let me see your glory," they say with Moses (Ex. 33:18).

It is not displeasing to God that we should look forward to the time, or eternity rather, when the faith we now have will be removed and give way to the vision of Christ in the state of glory. There have been saints who were blessed with a fleeting glimpse of the Divine while they were still in this life. We must not be afraid to want that which the saints wanted. We must not be afraid to ask God for great things, since His wealth is inexhaustible.

We must long for the time when the faith we now have will give way to sight, and shadow to substance. Heaven is a place where we won't have to exercise faith anymore—that is why it's so consoling to think of the time when we shall no longer have to be in this life. Faith is the road on which we go to heaven, and once there, we shall have attained to the knowledge of God we started out to seek by means of faith.

HOLD HEAVEN IN YOUR HAND

When I die, I shall be with the great Saint Teresa, and others like her, whom I love so much. Heaven is being with those who are already there, and in participating in their own fruitive bliss. We cannot think of heaven enough, this in spite of those who tell us that true spirituality consists in being riveted to this dreary land of exile we call the earth. God will come and take us to Himself. This will constitute our eternal life.

Our eternal life will consist in being with Jesus in the most complete and perfect way possible for a finite human being. God has destined us for Himself. It is for this reason He does not permit anything less than He is to satisfy us. Does not the Psalmist say, "On waking, I shall be content in your presence" (17:15)?

There are several ways these words can be rendered according to their original Hebrew, such as "I shall be satiated," etc., indicating that the full and perfect satisfaction of all our desires can only take place after our departure from this life. We should think of heaven day and night. That is the sole preoccupation worthy of a person redeemed by the blood of the God-Man. We cannot save ourselves. It's for this reason God came down from heaven. Day and night we should think of all our Lord has done for us by means of His Incarnation. Day and night we should have in mind the destiny for which we have been created by an infinitely good and knowing and loving Lord.

Was it not this thought of heaven and the infinite bliss we shall experience there that the Psalmist had in view when he tells us that he "delights" in the "law of the Lord" (Ps. 1:2)? Like the Psalmist, we too, should meditate on that "law," the infinitely beautiful one our Lord is. We should think of heaven day and night, since by so doing we are really calling to mind Him who has done so much for us—the God-Man.

The saints thought of Christ every single minute of the day. Our salvation lies in thinking of Jesus, and, in so doing, with all we are. Heaven, with the happiness that's there, is close by because He who is Lord thereof is always present in our hearts and minds. Christ, the infinite bliss He is, is always around. He is closer to us than we are to ourselves. We should think of this so that we may in that way be beatified. It's Jesus we want. It's Him we need to be eternally happy, and not anything else created by God.

The saints were Christ-minded people. To imitate them we must become what they have been. The saints thought of eternity all the time. They could not get the thought of it out of their hearts and minds. We must think of heaven all the time, seeing that as mortal creatures we shall soon be there. It's only a "little while," our Lord says to us, and we shall see Him.

We shall see Him in all His majesty and glory. Oh, how wonderful it is to think of Christ all the time! What sweetness of soul such thinking of Him brings with it! The saints could not contain themselves when they thought of the happiness that would be theirs as soon as they closed their eyes in death. To be happy as they had been we must ask for the grace to be what they have been. The saints could not get rid of the thought of heaven, and it was in this inability to get rid of it that all their happiness lay.

How happy the saints must have been all the time they found themselves in their mortal state! Should we not want to be as happy as they were? The happiness of the saints can only become our own by thinking of heaven day and night. The devil does not want us to think of the joys of the life to come. And so we should not listen to the diabolical insinuations he puts into our hearts along those lines. Having himself forfeited his eternal destiny, he wants us to do the same. The devil loves his own miserable state, and so he does all God allows him to get us to share his own unhappiness. We defeat the wiles of Satan by thinking of heaven all the time. The devil cannot have these joys, so he does all he can to stop us from having them. The devil does all he can to stop us from thinking of the joys of heaven—he does this by directing our thoughts to this world alone.

We should not "have a home in time," a great poet of our own day (Rilke) has said. How wonderful it is to think of heaven all the time and to have the joys that are there constantly before us! Can anything we do be more pleasing to God than the thought of being with Him in the state of glory?

There have always been those who say it is wrong to think of heaven all the time. They say we should limit the concern of our hearts to this brief existence in time, since that is the way to be practical. The saints were of an opposite opinion, and it's them to whom we have to listen if we wish to have our hearts filled with the peace of Christ and partake of His divine joys.

Can anyone be lost who thinks of heaven all the time? Can such a person be unhappy in this life? The answer is a resounding no. No one has ever been overcome with sorrow or despair who has made the thought of the joys of the life to come the mainstay of his earthly existence. We cannot be defeated in this life if we follow the injunction of Saint Paul to have "our conversation in heaven."

There is music in the air, and it comes to us when we think of the joys of the life to come. Earth drags downward, but the thought of heaven lifts the soul to its own divine heights. We must recreate ourselves in this life by our realization that we shall soon be where nothing harmful exists. We must think of heaven all the time, so that we may in that way become the "heavenized" human beings God wants us to be. In a limited way, God wants us to be what He Himself is. God wants us to love whatever He does and to rejoice in His own infinite bliss.

Will we accept His will along that line? If we do, we shall be eternally blessed. How foolish we are, not to let the thought of heaven dominate our lives! We would in that way have our heaven right here on earth—at least, the beginnings thereof. And isn't it the beginnings of heaven's bliss God wants for us to be living a true spiritual life?

By means of prayer, that bliss enters the soul. The devil is loose in the world; that's why the thought of heaven is absent from it. He plucks it from the hearts of men, so they may be as miserable as himself. "Myself am hell," the devil exclaims in John Milton's "Paradise Lost." By thinking of heaven all the time we shall avoid Satan's own miserable fate.

THE SWEETNESS OF THE CROSS

As a result of original sin, all things are signed with the sign of the Cross, and to get to God we have to suffer—there being no other way a human being is able to contact the divine. Before sin was committed, man was able to get to God without pain of any kind, but this process had been completely reversed. We can blame our first parents for the fact that we now have to suffer untold woes to get to know what the joys of heaven are like—we can get to know them even now but at the price of great anguish of body and mind. The majority of mankind, those outside the Church, persistently refuse to accept the doctrine of original sin. Yet, do what they may, they can in no way avoid experiencing the consequences of that sin in the form of all the sufferings a person has to go through in this life. The hospitals of the world are a mute witness to this fact.

Men dodge the truths of faith, but they cannot avoid the lot of their human mortality, with all of its unpleasant limitations. We cannot avoid pain, no matter what our attitude to the Church may be, the Church which teaches the truths about original sin, with all its consequences. Christ came to undo the effects of original sin, and He did so both as God and Man. He made atonement for that sin in His own Person—that is why we love Him so much and offer up to Him the entire homage of our heart and mind.

The world will never be fundamentally different from what it is now. To be convinced of this fact all we have to do is turn to the pages of history. We will quickly see that in all essentials man is no better off today than he has been in past ages. He still has to suffer a great deal in order to learn by personal experience what things divine are like and the kind of joys to be had by means of this suffering. Christ still points the way to the only true peace to be had on this earth, and that way is the way of the Cross—the Cross that has blessed and sanctified suffering in every single phase and detail of our human experience.

We have to suffer to know what true love is like and to taste the sweetness of it in the substance of our soul. Without this suffering, we remain dumb beasts as far as the things of our higher nature are concerned—it's these sufferings which render these things real and vivid to us. Has anything great ever been accomplished without pain and sorrow of every kind? The answer to this question can be had from those who created all the great masterpieces of art—they all came about through anguish of heart and mind of those by whom they were produced.

It's an axiom of human experience that all true greatness is born of pain, and so this fact renders the Cross of Christ so precious to us. It is written that when "Moses led Israel forward from the Red Sea ... . they arrived at Marah, where they could not drink the water, because it was too bitter. . . . As the people grumbled against Moses, saying, 'What are we to drink?' he appealed to the Lord, who pointed out to him a certain piece of wood. When he threw this into the water, the water became fresh (Hebrew, sweet)" (Exodus, 15:22-25). Now this "wood" was a figure of the Cross of Christ which renders sweet all the painful things we have to go through in this life. "What does he know who has not been tried?" it says in the Vulgate translation of the book of Sirach (34:9). It is in vain we will go searching elsewhere for the kind of knowledge suffering alone has the power to instill into us.

Everyone wants to be happy, but there are few who do not reject the sufferings by which alone this happiness can be produced in the soul. Suffering is bitter, but it leads to what is infinitely sweet, the sweetness of Christian spirituality. By the bitterness of the Cross He who is sweetness in essence changed the world.

We, too, can change our lives by embracing all God allows to happen to us. Thus, no matter how repugnant to the tastes and desires of our lower nature—suffering transmutes those tastes and these desires into what is supernatural and transcendent.

WHAT IS GOD? WHAT IS MAN?

We cannot comprehend the mystery of God for the same reason we cannot comprehend the mystery of our own being. These two mysteries being one and the same, we cannot think of God without thinking of what we ourselves are.

What am I? The answer to this question is countered by another in which we say, "What is God?" God is part of ourselves and we are part of Him. We cannot separate ourselves from God and look upon Him independently from our own being.

When we think of God and reflect on His attributes, we at the same time bring ourselves into consideration. We cannot divide the divine and the human. In a mystical way, we are one with God. "The Father and I are one" (John 10:30). It is possible for one raised to close union with the divine to say the same thing.

There is a mystical relationship between God and man. It is this which renders our thoughts about Him so marvelous and strange. What is God? What is man? Has there ever been a clear-cut answer to these two questions? Not in this life, but we may hope to get one in the world to come. Men torture themselves intellectually to find out what God is. To be logical, they should undergo the same amount of torture to find out what they themselves are!

We reach a stage in the spiritual life in which we are unable to think of ourselves apart from God—and of Him apart from ourselves. Perhaps it is in this that the whole significance of the Incarnation lies! Christ came that God and man may become one—not in essence, of course, but by means of grace. Heretics have erred in their effort to identify their own being with the divine Essence.

Saints are holy, but they are not God—only God is God. We rejoice at the thought that God alone is truly holy and that all others are the partakers of His own sanctity. Nearness to God will enable us to become truly holy, but never that which God alone will always be. There is no pantheism for a Catholic if he is faithful to the teachings of the Church. Error and heresy are for the children of Satan, but never for those who remain close to the bosom of the Church. We love God and strive to imitate the life of His divine Son. We are safe when we follow in the footsteps of Christ. The Church He founded is the Mother of sanctity—it's in her alone that the attainment of it is made possible.

We love ourselves when we get the grace to love Christ—love for Him constituting the innermost portion of our own being. Christ becomes the innermost self of everyone who has faith in Him. It's in the realization of this truth that our whole earthly consolation lies.

We have our Love in ourselves and it is this that matters from a supernatural point of view. "We love You, Jesus," becomes the motto of the saints. It's in the repetition of these words that our whole consolation lies.

When we are in danger we call upon the Holy Name of Jesus and we are rescued by it. We know by faith that we are always with God—He constituting our essential makeup. God constitutes the life of all the living and the reason in all reasonable beings. We cannot think unless God gives us the intelligence to do so. We cannot do anything without and apart from Him, sin alone excepted.

Without His permission we cannot even offend Him. The point is that nothing can be done without God. Without Him to sustain us, we cannot even exist. A marvelous relationship exists between the creature and the Creator of that creature, and it is in the realization of this relationship that drives the saints into ecstasy. They are beside themselves with wonder and awe when they reflect on all that God is to man. The saints can never take anything for granted. This is why they marvel at the sight of a human being. The saints stand in need of no signs or portents greater and more commonplace than nature herself. To them she is a continuous and uninterrupted miracle to be marveled at with wonder and awe.

The saint is never bored. He finds everything that exists an object of fascination. The saint sees God everywhere. He sees Him above all in his own inner being. Where is God? He is right here in ourselves. He exists even in the sinner, and it takes but faith to make him manifest. We know, of course, that that which is divine cannot be seen with the eyes of the body. However, the soul enlightened by faith has a way of apprehending that about which the senses know nothing. We can see God in God, but He is also present in the things which He has made. They bear the stamp and evidence of His workmanship. God has left traces of Himself in our own soul, and so we should, by means of reflection, seek Him there. There is a mystical affinity between our inner being and God, who brought it into existence—we cannot be without Him who always is.

We may spend years reading learned works, but learning is to know that God exists and to become intimately aware of Him in everything with which we are brought into intimate relationship. We have to ask for the grace to find God in ourselves—this is where He is most fully present.

How many become spiritually famished because they fail to seek the divine where it is nearest to them—in themselves? Such people fail to identify themselves with Christ. They seek the eternal and Substantial Good outside themselves.

'THE FOOL SAYS IN HIS HEART . . .'

Psalm 14:1

God is always with us. He is never far from us—if he were, we could cease to be that which, by means of Him, we are. In a certain sense, God is part of ourselves; that part of ourselves belonging completely to Him which, like Himself, will always continue to be. How foolish the atheists are in denying the existence of Him without whom they would not exist. The atheists have a false conception of divinity which prompts them to assert that God does not exist.

There is much falsehood and error in the world today, yet not only today because there was never a time in history when falsehood and error did not exist. There are so many false religions in the world now that it is important for men to pray for the grace to know where the true one is. It's a grace to be able to believe in God as He makes Himself manifest in His divine Son. There is so much misery in the world today, and it all springs from unbelief, from the erroneous conceptions men form of the divine Majesty.

In the ages gone by, God revealed Himself to the people of Israel, and He now continues to make Himself manifest by means of His Church. It is from her we have to learn Who and What God is, being, as she is meant to be, the teacher of the human race. The devil will always harbor hatred for the Church of Rome, since it is in her that men find the answers to all their questions pertaining to the Godhead. It was the devil who crucified our Lord, making use of human instruments by which this was to be done. The same devil it is who now hates the Church and does all allowed him by God to bring about her destruction. The devil is astute enough to realize that if he could get rid of the Church he could also uproot belief in the existence of God. Someone said that "those who attack the Catholic Church are like those who throw stones at the sun."

How pathetic such people are, and in what futility they end their lives, namely, trying to destroy the indestructible. God is with us all the time, though we may not always be conscious to know that He is around, upholding us in the existence we have by His power, goodness and love. We exist because God loves us. If He did not love us, we would never have been born.

Men are foolish in asking questions about God which God alone is able to answer, and to answer them in a way they could not comprehend in the present life. "Why is this?" and "Why is that?" we are always inclined to say in our ignorance. Such talk is foolish, seeing it is not God's will that we should now know the reason for things we shall have only when we get to heaven.

On earth, the reason for many of God's actions is shrouded in mystery, and so we have to believe that there is a reason for what seems to us unreasonable. Now, knowing that God knows this reason, we are content, our faith in Him tranquilizing and pacifying the soul. How can we hope to comprehend the infinite reasons God has for doing things with our finite minds? How can the finite grasp the infinite?

God is always around—though at times we feel Him not. God is invisibly present in all visible things, and, by means of His presence, sustains them in existence.

It is a grace to be able to believe in God, and so we have to dispose ourselves for it. It is not given to all because of their indisposition. "God's glory is increased," the great Saint Robert Bellarmine said, " . . . in that only they believe in Him whom He wishes should believe in Him." How good God is to give us the grace to be able both to love and believe in Him, since without this love and this belief we would be like the beasts of the field. Many there are who are like the lower animals because, through their own fault, they lack this love and this belief. Hell is a place where no one believes or loves.